Smoothies
& Juices

The Essential Recipe Handbook

Gina Steer

STAR FIRE

Contents

Delicious Juices

We all know that we need to improve our diets by eating more fruit and vegetables, and indeed, many people have taken this to heart and have already increased their intake. The World Health Organization recommends that we eat at least five portions of fruit and vegetables per day. However for some, this is not as easy as it sounds, due to lifestyle, taste or even economics.

Life is hectic for many people and often involves eating on the go, grabbing a bite as we rush from place to place and seldom managing to eat healthily. There is also a question of taste. We may not like some or all vegetables or even fruit. Children in particular are often fussy and 'picky' eaters, and sometimes when they say 'I don't like this' it is easier just to take it away and not force the issue. In addition, fresh fruits and vegetables can sometimes be expensive, pushing the family budget too high.

This is where fruit juices and smoothies are the perfect answer. You can make healthy and delicious drinks, with no added extras such as sugar, colourings or preservatives out of one or two fruits or vegetables for next to nothing. These will still provide a delicious drink crammed full of

vitamins, minerals and fibre. The fruits and vegetables used for juicing need not be uniform and perfect in size, as long as they are undamaged by bruising or are not going rotten. They will work perfectly, with an added benefit of being ready in no time at all – ideal for when the children come in tired and thirsty or you need a quick energy boost. What could be better than to juice an orange, ready in a couple of minutes? So quick and easy. As an added bonus, the drink will be crammed full of goodness with no nasty additives present.

This book contains a comprehensive collection of recipes ranging from simple fruit or vegetable juices and delicious, creamy smoothies, to drinks designed to lift and revitalize, others to help in healthy detoxification, and some rather more decadent cocktails and punches, both with and without alcohol. There really is something for everyone here, and if you have never juiced you will soon become a convert. Quick and easy, juicing is an ideal way to get or stay healthy.

This book aims to help everyone by providing speedy, simple ideas that are full of essential nutrients and taste delicious. Adapt the recipes to suit your taste, substituting ingredients if necessary. After a couple of weeks you will be happily juicing and smoothing at every opportunity.

Smashing Smoothies

Smoothies are a fairly recent innovation and are a creamy, long drink often with two to four ingredients as well as fruit or vegetables. They are an ideal way of getting children and fussy adults to consume fruit and vegetables. They can also be quickly and easily used to counteract the stresses of modern day life, with the addition of herbs or natural remedies. They are the ultimate drink for an immediate energy boost.

One of the biggest benefits of consuming fruit is the advantage it gives you in the fight against cancer and heart disease, two of the biggest killers in the twenty–first century throughout the western world. Many fruits contain antioxidants, a vital component against these problems. Fruit and vegetables can also give you extra natural energy as well as keeping your immune system alert and strong. So it really does make sense to include more of these vital ingredients in your diet and that of your family. What better way than in a refreshing smoothie?

One way to make a smoothie is to use a smoothie machine, but a blender or food processor will work just as well, although it may take a little longer. A juicer will also get the desired results, but you will need the addition of a whisk and large container to get the best results.

When it comes to ingredients that are suitable for using in smoothies, there are very few limits, especially with fruits. Most fruits are suitable providing they are ripe and juicy and have been prepared by the removal of hard, tough skin and seeds. With vegetables it

is more a question of personal taste than the vegetable itself, as most can be made into a delicious, if unusual, drink. Herbs and spices can also be incorporated into a smoothie. If using herbs, many of which have great health benefits, remember to check that they are thoroughly cleaned with no aphids or other creepy crawlies. Spices with hard outer casing will need either pounding or cracking open in a pestle and mortar to release the seeds. The little pieces of casing that may be left should sink to the bottom of the goblet and so can be avoided.

In this book we have put together a huge variety of smoothie ideas, ranging from those that help in a healthy lifestyle to those that are bordering on the decadent. The recipes are designed for maximum enjoyment – even those that are aimed at detoxifying or revitalizing. There is no point in producing a drink that no one will drink, no matter how healthy. Drinks, like foods, should be enjoyed, and it is an added bonus if they are doing you good.

Equipment & Techniques

These days we enjoy a vast array of fruit and vegetables ranging from home-grown varieties to tropical produce. In order to be able to prepare and make the recipes in this book, it would be useful to own certain pieces of equipment.

Juicer

This is a simple machine that will extract the juice from fruit or vegetables while leaving the skin, pulp, seeds and debris behind. All fruits and vegetables can be juiced, including parsnips, carrots, cabbage, beetroots, apples, pineapples, oranges and melons.

Juicers come in three types:

Centrifugal

All of either fruit or vegetables are fed into the machine on to a fast spinning grater. The juice is forced through small holes in the grater while the peel, seeds, etc. stay in the grater or are sent to a waste container that can be emptied when finished. Normally a jug or cup-type container is supplied with the machine.

Masticating

Here the fruit and or vegetables are ground up into a pulp before being forced through a wire mesh with great force. These tend to be quite pricey, but more juice is produced than with a centrifugal machine.

Hydraulic

Here the fruit and vegetables are chopped and crushed with revolving cutters. They are the most efficient of all, producing the maximum amount of juice, but also the most expensive.

Smoothie machine

These are similar in style to a blender, having a high-sided base where the engine is located and a goblet which has a non-drip pouring spout attached about one third up from the base. It has tough, durable blades, designed especially for crushing ice and chopping the foods. A pusher is included to ensure that everything is ground and chopped, and they have four push-control buttons. They work efficiently and quickly, producing delicious smoothies in minutes. The goblet has useful measures so you can see at a glance how much you have made. They can be hard to clean, however, and the liquid produced tends to be very thick. It is recommended that you add 300 ml/½ pint liquid (water or juice) to drinks made in this way. Add it early on, along with the first ingredients so that it sits in the bottom of the machine.

Blender

This can also be called a food processor or liquidizer, and consists of a base machine and a goblet with sturdy chopping blades. Often the goblet has the measurements up the sides and is ideal for soft fruits and vegetables, as well as blending juices with other ingredients. Here, the fruits and vegetables need to be prepared a little more by removing inedible parts, such as stalks, peel, seeds and tough skins. They have speed settings, so look for one that has a good range – many now offer a pulse button, which is an excellent addition.

Lemon squeezer

The simple lemon squeezer that most people have in their kitchen is vital for making juices and smoothies. It is ideal for squeezing all citrus fruits and is available in a variety of materials: glass, plastic, wood and aluminium.

Citrus presser

This is a more powerful lemon/citrus squeezer and consists of a glass jug with a lemon squeezer sitting on top and a handle at the side. It is operated by simply placing half a citrus fruit on the squeezer, pulling down the handle, which operates a rod, that presses out the juice into the jug. It is worth investing in if you plan to make a lot of juices.

Cooks' knife

Good knives are essential in the preparation of all food. For these recipes, you need one with a large, study blade – essential for cutting large, tough vegetables into portions and also for chopping herbs and fruits. You will also need a couple of other knives: a medium knife which is ideal for cutting fruits such as melon or pineapple, plus of course, a small vegetable knife, invaluable for preparing both fruit and vegetables.

Vegetable peeler

This is also extremely useful. I prefer a swivel peeler as it quick and easy to use and only removes a minimal amount of peel or skin, thus helping to preserve the nutrients.

Sturdy chopping board

This is needed both for cutting the fruit and vegetables and for preserving your work surfaces. Do keep a separate chopping board for fruit and vegetables, one for meat and one for fish. It is important to keep all your equipment scrupulously clean, so dishwasher safe utensils are a great investment.

As with many things, preparation is often the key to ensuring that a good result is achieved when making smoothies and juices. First, ensure that you have the correct machine for the type of drink that you are wishing to make. Once you have this, you are halfway there, but there are a few other pointers that will help you to produce delicious, nutritious drinks.

- First of all, whichever machine you have, do read the instruction booklet that accompanies it. Each machine will have slightly different applications and instructions, so for a perfect result read the booklet first and adapt the recipe if need be.

- Sometimes when making a drink it will come through too thick or even too thin – both are easy to rectify. If too thick, stir in some extra liquid or crushed ice; if too thin, pass extra fruit or vegetables through the machine and stir into the drink.

- Both fruit and vegetables are better if kept in the refrigerator before using, as this keeps them fresh and enhances their flavour. Always use plump, ripe produce.

- Frost the rim of a glass by rubbing a little citrus juice or water round the rim and dipping in caster sugar, or even salt for a 'sour'.

- Alternatively, you could add extra pieces of fruit or vegetables, cut into shapes if liked, and wedge on the rim of the glass. Try thinly paring a long strip of citrus rind and hanging from the rim.

- Be adventurous and experiment. Once you are used to your machine, make up your own concoctions and enjoy blending different ingredients with herbs and spices.

Ingredients

When it comes to preparing vegetables, it is recommended to peel root vegetables such as carrots and parsnips, but this is a personal choice and not strictly necessary.

- Cut off and discard the root if applicable as well as the leaf end and cut into chunks that will easily fit into the machine's goblet.
- All vegetables, but green vegetables in particular, should be thoroughly washed and allowed to drain.
- Vegetables should be firm and in good condition, certainly not going rotten and any bruised parts discarded.
- Use as fresh as possible, as the older the produce the less of the valuable nutrients it will contain.

The same applies to fruits.

- Use firm, sound fruits, but do ensure that they are ripe. Under-ripe fruits will be lacking in taste, flavour and aroma.
- Citrus fruits are better if peeled and the bitter white pith discarded.
- Stones and seeds should be discarded and where applicable the fruits should be rinsed and allowed to drain.
- Fruits such as apples and pears can be left unpeeled if preferred, but do discard the core.
- Melons should be skinned and the seeds discarded.
- Pomegranates are better if the flesh and seeds are sieved before using.
- Soft berries such as raspberries should be picked over and leaves or hulls discarded. Lightly rinse before using.

Vegetables

Beetroot

Use either raw or cooked but not soaked in vinegar. Reputed to help kidney function. Contains folate vitamin, potassium and magnesium.

Broccoli

Use raw. High in fibre and vitamin C, beta-carotene and antioxidants. An important food in the fight against cancer and heart disease.

Carrot

Peel before using. Rich source of beta-carotene, which converts in the body to vitamin A (good for vision) plus a good antioxidant.

Celery

Wash thoroughly before use. Helps to lower blood pressure.

Chilli

Handle with care and when preparing avoid touching sensitive parts of the body such as the eyes. Wash hands thoroughly after use. Contains antioxidants, is good for stimulating the metabolic rate and helps to lower blood cholesterol levels. Also contains high levels of capsaicin a natural painkiller.

Courgette

Trim and peel before use. Member of the squash family. Low in calories and a good smoothie base due to high water content.

Cucumber

Part of the squash family. Comes in two varieties – hothouse, the most common, and ridge, a shorter variety with small spikes on the ridged skin. Can act as a mild diuretic and photochemical that can help reduce cholesterol levels in the blood.

Fennel

Also called Florence fennel. Wash thoroughly, discarding the root. Leafy tops can be used as garnish. Contains small amounts of beta-carotene and potassium.

Okra

Also called Lady's Fingers. Trim off the tops before using and use within 1–2 days of purchase. Contains seeds inside the vegetable which are used as a thickener in Creole dishes. Very good source of soluble fibre, good for lowering cholesterol levels.

Parsnip

Peel and discard top before use and cut into chunks. Flesh has a sweet flavour. Contains a moderate amount of fibre, beta-carotene, vitamin B1, and niacin, essential with the other B vitamins for growth and a healthy nervous system.

Peppers: green, red and yellow

Green peppers are one of the best vegetable sources of vitamin C. All peppers are high in beta-carotene as well as rich in vitamin C. As with chillies, all are high in capsaicin, a natural painkiller, and reputed to be helpful in alleviating the pain from arthritis.

Sweet potato

Peel before use. Normally an orange-fleshed tuber, rich in beta-carotene (the white fleshed sweet potato is not). Both varieties contain good quantities of vitamins C and E and are a great source of slow-release carbohydrates.

Tomato

Comes in many different shapes, sizes and colours. A rich source of lycopene, an important antioxidant in the prevention of heart disease and cancer. Also contain beta-carotene and vitamins C and E.

Fruits

Apple

Eaters and cookers, normally kept for cooking, come in a many varieties. Choose firm, unblemished fruits with plenty of juice. Contain vitamin C. No need to peel but core first.

Apricot

Small, orange coloured stone fruit with a slightly hairy, edible skin. Needs stoning. High in beta-carotene. Very sweet, especially when dried.

Banana

Skin is green when under-ripe and turns yellow on ripening. Rich in vitamin B6 and C. Popular food as easily eaten and digested. Peel before using.

Blackberry

Grown both wild and cultivated and contains significant amounts of vitamin E, flavonoids and ellagic acid which helps to block cancer cells. Rinse lightly before using.

Blackcurrant

Rich source of vitamin C and the anti-cancer carotenoid lutein. Grown extensively for commercial juicing rather than sold as fruit. Strip from the stalks, rinse and use.

Blueberry

Small blue/black berries grown in the USA, Italy and France. Rinse before using. Highly nutritious and good in the fight against cancer, especially when dried.

Coconut

Large fruit with a hard, hairy outer casing or husk. To remove from the outer casing, bash with a mallet to reveal the inner fruit. Pierce this carefully to drain off the coconut milk. Coconut is high in saturated fat, although many believe that this fat is not as harmful as animal or dairy saturated fats.

Fig

Grown extensively in Mediterranean countries, coming in red, green and purple varieties. Can be eaten fresh or dried. Wash fresh figs before using. Contain small amount of carbohydrate and beta-carotene.

Grapefruit

Three varieties are available: pink, red and yellow, with yellow being the most common and also more tart than the other two. Contains good amounts of vitamin C. Peel and discard the bitter white pith before using.

Grapes

Come in three colours: green, red and black, both seedless and seeded. Red grapes contain polyphenols, also found in red wine, which help in the fight against heart disease, and some research shows it can help against cancer.

Kiwi fruit

Grown extensively in New Zealand and now available in both green and gold varieties. Small fruits with a brown, slightly hairy skin, the flesh containing tiny edible black seeds. Peel before using. A rich source of vitamin C.

Mango

Grown extensively in India as well as the Caribbean and other tropical countries. A green/yellow smooth skin with bright orange flesh around a large stone. Peel, cut off the flesh and use raw. Very rich in fibre, especially soluble fibre. Helps to keep cholesterol low and also contains vitamin E and antioxidants. Leave until ripe before using.

Melon

About five varieties readily available with perhaps the most popular one being honeydew with bright yellow skin and pale flesh. Other varieties include ogen, cantaloupe, gallia and watermelon.

Orange

Rich in vitamin C and flavonoids, which have a good antioxidant effect on the body. Peel, discarding the bitter white pith before using.

Papaya

An elongated fruit with a green skin that turns yellow as it ripens. Rich in beta-carotene and an excellent source of soluble fibre, which aids digestion.

Passion fruit

Small, dark purple fruit that wrinkles once ripe. Both the flesh and seeds are edible. Contains vitamin C.

Peach/nectarine

Both members of the same family. Flesh is normally yellow but a white flesh variety is occasionally available during the summer months. Contain vitamin C and a trace of soluble fibre.

Pear

Many English varieties available including Williams, Conference and Comice. Normally picked under-ripe and allowed to ripen slowly. Contain vitamin C and potassium.

Pineapple

Grown in most tropical and subtropical countries. The attractive plume needs discarding before eating, as does the skin and hard central core. Contains bromelain which aids digestion, breaking down protein and making it easier to digest.

Plum

Many different varieties, including Victoria, Czar, damsons and greengages. All are an excellent source of fibre, with the red-skinned varieties containing beta-carotene.

Just Juice

We all know how important it is that we maintain a healthy lifestyle, and an integral part of doing this is to eat plenty of fruit and vegetables. Many of us live life to the full and tend to grab a takeaway or pick up quick and easy convenience food. Here you have the perfect combination: quick and healthy snacks ready in seconds and guaranteed to keep you fit. This chapter deals with easy-to-make juices, from a Citrus Crush with three different citrus fruits and juices crammed full of summer berries, to more exotic concoctions with passion fruit, mango and papaya.

Vegetables have not been overlooked and provide a brilliant way to get children to eat their veg. You can choose from a simple carrot juice, beetroot juiced with apple or orange and others that use celery, peppers and even broccoli. Just remember that if you use a juicer, you will get a thinner juice than if you use a blender. Whether using a juicer or a blender, it is important make sure that some liquid is added if the foods being juiced are firm in texture.

Juices are the perfect answer for the whole family to get and stay fit and healthy. So get juicing!

Citrus Crush

Citrus fruits are full of vitamin C and as the body does not store this vitamin, a daily glass of this crush will keep the levels up and help to prevent colds.

Ingredients

1 pink grapefruit

2 satsumas

1 lime

chilled mineral water to dilute, optional

ice cubes to serve

lemon slice to decorate

Method

Peel the grapefruit, satsumas and lime, discarding any pips and divide into segments. Pass through a juicer or blender until the juice is formed. Dilute with the iced mineral water if using. Pour into glasses, add ice cubes if liked and serve. Decorate the glasses with a lime slice.

Alternative If a slightly sweeter drink is preferred, add a little clear honey before juicing.

Kiwi Fruit Whizz

It is now possible to get both green and golden kiwi fruits, and they offer one of the best sources of vitamin C. They are best eaten when the fruit yields slightly when lightly pressed.

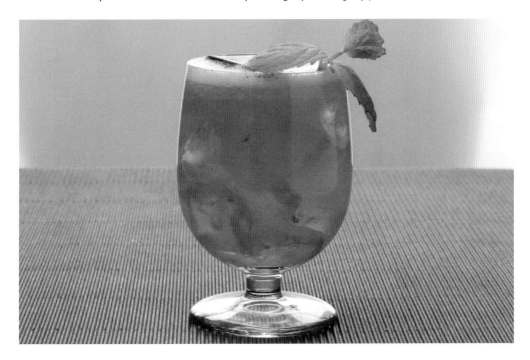

Ingredients

2 green kiwi fruits
1 golden kiwi fruit
1 red apple, rinsed
150 ml/¹/₄ pint sparkling water to dilute, optional
ice cubes to serve
apple slices to decorate

Method

Peel the kiwi fruits and chop into large pieces. Cut the apple into quarters and core. Reserve 2–4 slices and roughly chop the remainder. Pass the prepared fruits through a juicer or blender until the juice is formed. Pour into tall glasses and dilute with the water if using. Add ice cubes and decorate the glasses with the apple slices. Serve immediately.

Alternative If liked, use either green or gold kiwi fruits and add 1 small peeled orange in place of the apple. Decorate with kiwi fruit slices.

Pomelo and Orange Crush

Pomelos are the largest of the citrus fruits and are similar to grapefruits in both look and taste. They have an extremely thick skin and a bitter, fibrous pulp.

Ingredients

1 pomelo
2 large oranges
1–2 tsp clear honey or to taste
chilled mineral water to dilute, optional

Method

Peel the pomelo, ensuring that all the bitter white pith is discarded. Cut off and reserve two thin slices from one of the oranges. Peel both oranges, discarding the white pith and add to the pomelo flesh. Pass through a juicer or blender until the juice is formed. Stir in the honey to taste and pour into glasses. Dilute with water if using, decorate the glasses with the reserved orange slices and serve.

Alternative Use other citrus fruits if pomelo is not available and dilute with sparkling water.

Ugli Juice

Ugli fruits are similar to grapefruit and are, in fact, a cross between a grapefruit and a tangerine. They are sweeter in taste than the yellow grapefruit, similar to the pink variety. They are quite difficult to find, so snap them up when in season.

Ingredients

1 ugli fruit
1 wedge ripe honeydew melon
few black seedless grapes
chilled sparkling water to dilute
extra grapes to decorate, optional

Method

Peel the ugli fruit, discarding the peel and pith. Cut the flesh into chunks. Remove any seeds from the melon and discard the skin. Cut into chunks and add to the ugli. Pass through a juicer or blender until the juice is formed. Pour into glasses and dilute with water, if using. Decorate the glasses with a few grapes by hanging little bunches over the rim of the glass.

Alternative Use either pink or red grapefruit if ugli fruit is not available, and if preferred, strain through a fine sieve to give a smooth juice.

Apple and Raspberry Juice

This juice can be made using either fresh or thawed frozen raspberries. If using thawed frozen raspberries, you may find that it produces a little more juice than fresh.

Ingredients

2 eating apples, such as Golden Delicious
225 g/8 oz fresh or thawed frozen raspberries
150 ml/¼ pint orange juice
ice cubes
chilled sparkling water to dilute, optional
sprigs of mint to decorate

Method

Cut the apples into quarters and discard the cores. Chop into chunks. Pass through a juicer or blender with the raspberries and orange juice (if using a blender) until the juice is formed. Stir in the orange juice if not already used, then pour over ice cubes in glasses and dilute with sparkling water if using. Float a mint sprig on top and serve.

Alternative Add a mixture of berries to the apples – try blackberries, strawberries or blueberries.

Berry Juice

Berries such as strawberries, blueberries, blackberries and raspberries are available all year round so there is no need to keep this delicious juice just for the summer months. Strawberries are an excellent source of vitamin C, while raspberries and blackberries are high in fibre and blueberries are reputed to have anti-carcinogenic

Ingredients

175 g/6 oz ripe strawberries
100 g/4 oz ripe raspberries
50 g/2 oz ripe blackberries
chilled mineral water to dilute, optional
ice cubes to serve

Method

Hull the strawberries, rinse and cut in half. Lightly rinse the raspberries and blackberries. Pass through a juicer or blender until the juice is formed. Place the ice cubes into glasses, pour over the juice, dilute to taste with the water if using and serve immediately.

Alternative Use each fruit separately to make a single flavoured juice.
Dilute with iced water if liked in place of the ice cubes. If left for a little while, the juices may need stirring before drinking.

25

Spinach

These days we can buy a good variety of melons throughout the year. These range from the red–fleshed watermelon, orange–fleshed charentais, light green ogen and the slightly paler green honeydew, to the similarly pale green to golden gallia and the fragrant orange–fleshed cantaloupe. Vary the juice according to taste and availability.

Ingredients

1 wedge ripe honeydew melon
1 wedge ripe cantaloupe melon
1 wedge ripe ogen melon
small piece root ginger, peeled and grated
chilled mineral water to dilute, optional
ice cubes to serve
redcurrants to decorate

Method

Discard any seeds from the melon wedges and cut off the skin. Cut the flesh into chunks and pass through a juicer or blender together with the ginger until the juice is formed. Pour into tall glasses, dilute with mineral water, if using, and add ice cubes. Drape a redcurrant sprig over the side and serve immediately.

Alternative Add 2–3 peeled and seeded clementines to the melons prior to juicing and use a few segments to decorate the glasses.

Melon with Passion Fruit Juice

Passion fruits are at their best when they are at their ugliest. They need to be very wrinkled – if smooth, the fruit will be under-ripe and the wonderful aromatic flavour and aroma will not be at its best.

Ingredients

2 wedges honeydew melon
1 wedge ogen melon
2 ripe passion fruits
chilled sparkling water to dilute, optional
ice cubes to serve

Method

Discard any seeds from the melon wedges and remove the skin. Cut the flesh into chunks. Scoop out the flesh and seeds from one and a half of the passion fruits and add to the melon flesh. Pass through a juicer or blender until the juice is formed. Pour into glasses. Add sparkling water to dilute, if using, and add ice cubes. Scoop out the seeds from the remaining half of passion fruit and spoon on top of the juices. Serve immediately.

Alternative Use the flesh and seeds of three passion fruits in the juice and top the glasses of juice with a teaspoonful of finely chopped melon flesh.

Peach Juice with Orange and Plum

Peaches or nectarines can be used in this recipe, depending on what is available. Look for the white–fleshed varieties, which are around in the summer. They have a more delicate flavour and often contain more juice.

Ingredients

4 ripe peaches
4 ripe plums, such as Victoria plums
1 large orange
chilled sparkling water to dilute, optional
ice cubes to serve

Method

Cut the peaches and plums in half and discard the stones. Rinse lightly then cut into chunks. Peel the orange, discarding the bitter white pith and any pips. Divide into segments and add to the peaches and plums. Pass through a juicer or blender until the juice is formed. Pour into glasses and dilute with water if liked. Add ice cubes and serve.

Alternative Omit the orange and add 1–2 drops of almond essence
to the peaches and plums before blending.

Mango and Orange Juice

Mangos provide an excellent source of antioxidant carotenoids and are extremely rich in soluble fibre and a good source of vitamin E. Buy mangos a few days before they are required, as they are best eaten fully ripe.

Ingredients

2 large, ripe mangos
2 large oranges
chilled sparkling water to dilute, optional
ice cubes to serve
thinly pared orange rind to decorate

Method

Peel the mangos and cut the flesh away from the large stone. Cut the flesh into chunks. Using a vegetable peeler, carefully pare off two long thin strips of orange rind and reserve. Peel the remaining rind and bitter white pith off both oranges and divide into segments. Discard the pips and add to the mangos. Pass through a juicer or blender until the juice is formed. Pour into glasses, dilute with water if using and add ice cubes. Drape the orange rind down the sides of the glass and serve.

Alternative Canned mangos can be used if ripe ones are not available. Drain before using.
Ripe papayas can also be used, but discard the skin and black seeds before juicing.

Tropical Fruit Juice

It is important to ensure that the fruits to be juiced are at their best and perfectly ripe. If beginning to bruise, the fruits may be over-ripe and the flavour will not be as good.

Ingredients

1 ripe mango
1 papaya
1 ripe passion fruit
$^1/_2$ medium pineapple
chilled mineral water to dilute, optional
ice cubes to serve

Method

Peel the mango and cut the flesh away from the stone. Discard the peel and seeds from the papaya and cut into chunks. Add to the mango. Remove the plume and skin from the pineapple and cut lengthways into four.Discard the hard central core from the pineapple and cut into chunks. Reserve 2–4 pieces of pineapple and add the remainder to the mango and papaya. Pass through a juicer or blender until the juice is formed. Pour into glasses and dilute with water if using. Add ice cubes and decorate the glasses with the reserved pineapple. Serve.

Alternative For a thicker, creamier juice, add 1 large ripe peeled banana before juicing.

Pear and Raspberry Juice

As with all fruits, it is important when eating pears that they are ripe. Otherwise, pears especially lack taste and their texture is woody. Which variety you choose is often a question of taste and familiarity. Unlike many fruits, pears are not normally sold ripe but need to ripen at home. This can take as long as one week but is well worth the wait.

Ingredients

2 ripe pears, such as Conference or Comice
1 medium orange
100 g/4 oz fresh or thawed frozen raspberries
chilled mineral water to dilute, optional
ice cubes to serve
1 tsp flaked chocolate, optional

Method

Peel and core the pears, then peel the orange, discarding the bitter white pith, and divide into segments. Lightly rinse the raspberries if using fresh and add to the pears. Pass through a juicer or blender until the juice is formed. Pour into glasses, dilute with water, if using, and add ice cubes. If feeling extra indulgent, sprinkle the tops of each with a little crumbled flaked chocolate

Alternative Omit the raspberries and add the flesh and seeds of 3 ripe passion fruits. Whizz until blended then pass through a fine sieve to remove the seeds.

Red Grape Juice with Apple

Juice made from red grapes contains the same properties as red wine – polyphenols, an antioxidant and a powerful aid against heart disease, and ellagic acid which has cancer-fighting properties. Both excellent reasons to make this one of your favourites!

Ingredients

175 g/6 oz red seedless grapes
2 green apples
2 tbsp orange juice
chilled sparkling water to dilute, optional
ice cubes to serve

Method

Remove the grapes from their stalks and rinse lightly. Cut the apples into quarters and discard the cores. Rinse if not peeling, then cut into chunks. Add to the grapes together with the orange juice and pass through a juicer or blender until the juice is formed. Pour into glasses and dilute with the water, if using. Add ice cubes, stir and serve.

Alternative Use this juice as the basis for a non-alcoholic Pimms. Pour half the amount of juice into a jug and add some ice cubes. Add pieces of chopped fruits, such as apples, pears, strawberries, peaches and cucumber and top up with lemonade. Allow to stand for 5 minutes then stir and serve.

Pineapple and Orange Juice

When using pineapples to make juice it is imperative that the fruit is perfectly ripe. To check for ripeness, the fruit should have a good aroma and the leaves from the plume should come away when lightly pulled. Avoid over–ripe or damaged fruits.

Ingredients

1 large, ripe pineapple
4 tbsp orange juice
chilled sparkling water to serve
ice cubes to serve

Method

Place the pineapple onto a board and cut off and discard the plume and base. Standing the fruit upright, carefully cut away the skin with a sharp knife and discard. Cut the fruit lengthways into four wedges and discard the hard central core. Cut into chunks. Pass through a juicer or blender until the juice is formed. Stir in the orange juice, pour into glasses, dilute with the sparkling water, add ice cubes and serve.

Alternative Omit the orange juice and for a little extra sweetness add 1–2 tablespoons of clear honey.

Guava and Mango Juice

Guavas can be bought fresh or canned, but wherever possible do use fresh. If using canned, drain well before use. Guavas should be used ripe, so look for fruits that have a light yellow skin and yield when pressed lightly with the fingers.

Ingredients

4 ripe guavas

1 large, ripe mango

1–2 tsp clear honey, optional

chilled mineral water to dilute, optional

Method

Peel the guavas, discard the seeds and chop into chunks. Peel the mango and cut the flesh away from the stone. Chop and add to the guavas. Pass through a juicer or blender until the juice is formed. Taste and, if liked, add a little honey. Pour into tall glasses and dilute with water if using, stir and serve.

Alternative Replace the mango with one large, ripe, peeled, seeded papaya and in place of the iced water, place ice cubes in the glasses and pour the juice over before serving.

Orange and Pomegranate Juice

Pomegranates are one of the few fruits that are not available all year round, so take advantage of them when in season – normally around Christmas time.

Ingredients

3 large oranges
2 pomegranates
chilled mineral water to dilute, optional
ice cubes to serve

Method

Peel the oranges, discarding the bitter white pith, and cut the flesh into chunks. Cut the pomegranates in half and scoop out all the seeds. Reserve a few seeds if liked for decoration. Place the seeds with the oranges and pass through a juicer or blender until juiced. Place some ice cubes in the glasses and pour over the juice. Dilute with water if using. Scatter with the reserved pomegranate seeds and serve.

Alternative   Replace the oranges with two wedges of honey dew melon.
Remove the seeds and skin, chop into small chunks and blend with the pomegranate.

Sharon and Peach Juice

Sharon fruits, or persimmon, their original name, are not the best fruits to eat raw if they are not ripe. However, once ripe, they are very sweet and juicy and it is well worth waiting for the fruit to ripen.

Ingredients

3 ripe Sharon fruits
2 ripe peaches or nectarines
chilled mineral water to serve

Method

Discard the stalk from the Sharon fruits, rinse lightly and chop. Lightly rinse the peaches or nectarines, cut in half and discard the stones. Cut a few thin slices for decoration and reserve, cutting the remainder into chunks. Add to the Sharon fruits and pass through a juicer or blender until the juice is formed. Dilute with the water and pour into glasses. Decorate the glasses with the reserved peach slices and serve immediately.

Alternative   Replace the iced water with 150 ml/$^1/_4$ pint orange juice.

Apple and Blackberry Juice

Apples and blackberries must be one of the most popular combinations of fruits, but they are rarely used for juices. Look for large, plump blackberries that are bursting with flavour and juice.

Ingredients

2 large eating apples
225 g/8 oz ripe blackberries
1–2 tsp clear honey, optional
chilled sparkling water to dilute, optional
iced cubes to serve
2 mint sprigs

Method

Lightly rinse the apples and blackberries. Cut the apples into quarters, discard the core, cut into chunks and add to the blackberries. Pass through a juicer or blender until the juice is formed. Taste and add the honey if liked. Place the ice cubes in glasses, pour over the juice, dilute with water if using, decorate with a mint sprig and serve.

Alternative Replace the blackberries with the same amount of ripe blackcurrants. You may need to increase the amount of honey, depending on how ripe the blackcurrants are.

Blueberry and Raspberry Juice

Blueberries are very small, dark blue fruits, full of nutritional benefits. Juicing them gives a really deep blue juice, full of flavour and goodness.

Ingredients

300 g/10 oz ripe blueberries
175 g/6 oz fresh or thawed frozen raspberries
1 medium orange
chilled mineral water to dilute, optional

Method

Rinse the blueberries and raspberries if fresh. Peel the orange, discarding the skin and bitter white pith, divide into segments and add to the blueberries. Pass through a juicer or blender until the juice is formed. Pour into glasses, dilute with iced water if using and serve.

Alternative Use two large oranges in place of the raspberries and if wanted omit the honey.

Watermelon with Ginger

When using ginger with juices, it is recommended that you use fresh root ginger rather than powdered, as a far better flavour is achieved. Use a small sharp knife to peel the ginger and cut into small chunks.

Ingredients

1 large wedge watermelon
small piece fresh root ginger
1 lemon grass stalk
ice cubes to serve

Method

Discard the skin and pips from the watermelon and cut into chunks. Peel the root ginger, chop and add to the melon. Discard the outer leaves from the lemon grass, chop and add to the melon. Pass through a juicer or blender until the juice is formed. Place ice cubes into tall glasses, pour in the juice and serve.

Alternative Add the juice and flesh from two limes in place of the lemon grass stalk.
If a sweeter juice is preferred, add a little clear honey.

Carrot and Orange Juice

Carrots and oranges are a popular blend of flavours and offer a very healthy choice. The resulting juice is full of vitamin C from the oranges as well as flavonoids, which have antioxidant properties. Carrots also contain a rich source of beta-carotene as well as vitamin A.

Ingredients

225 g/8 oz carrots
2 large oranges
3–4 tbsp mineral water to blend, optional
chilled mineral water to dilute, optional

Method

Peel the carrots and chop into chunks. Peel and discard the bitter white pith from the oranges and divide into segments. Pass the carrots and orange segments through a juicer or blender until the juice is formed. If using a blender, add 3–4 tablespoons of water when blending. Pour into tall glasses, diluting with water if using and serve.

Alternative Increase the amount of carrots to 450 g/1 lb and omit the oranges.
Use 150 ml/$^1/_4$ pint chilled mineral water if using a blender. Use large carrots for speed rather than baby carrots.

Carrot and Red Grapefruit Juice

Red grapefruit tend to be available all year round these days. If you do have trouble finding them, however, use either pink or the more traditional yellow variety.

Ingredients
300 g/10 oz ripe carrots
2 red grapefruit
3–4 tbsp mineral water to blend, optional
chilled mineral water to dilute, optional
ice cubes to serve

Method
Peel the carrots, cut into chunks and reserve. Peel the grapefruits, discard the bitter white pith and divide into segments. Add the segments to the carrots and pass through a juicer or blender – with the water if using a blender – until the juice is formed. Pour the juice into glasses, dilute with water if using, add ice cubes and serve.

Alternative Add 3–4 tablespoons of natural bio yogurt to the juice for a great breakfast wake-up call.

Carrot, Beetroot and Apple

You can, if you wish, use cooked beetroot in this juice – it is easier and quicker to use than raw and will yield slightly more juice.

Ingredients

225 g/8 oz carrots

100 g/4 oz beetroot (see note above)

2 Granny Smith apples

1 celery stick or $\frac{1}{2}$ tsp celery salt (or to taste)

chilled mineral water to dilute, optional

ice cubes to serve, optional

celery sticks for stirring

Method

Peel the carrots and cut into chunks. Peel the beetroot, discarding the root and stalks, and cut into chunks. Cut the apples into quarters, discard the cores and chop roughly. Add to the carrot and beetroot, along with the trimmed, washed and chopped celery stick, if using. Pass through a juicer or blender until the juice is formed, adding celery salt to taste if wanted. Pour into glasses, dilute with the water if using, add ice cubes and serve with a celery stick for stirring.

Alternative Omit the apple and celery salt and replace with three celery stalks that have been trimmed, washed and chopped.

Tomato Juice

Tomato juice must be the most well-known and popular of all vegetable juices. Apart from being a staple juice which can be used in many different ways, it can also have many different vegetables added to it, giving a vast array of flavours which will suit most tastes. Try doing a little experimenting of your own – by adding chilli, garlic, herbs, curry-style spices, vegetables or even some fruits.

Ingredients

450 g/1 lb ripe tomatoes

pinch of sugar

chilled mineral water to dilute, optional

ice cubes to serve

twist of lemon, optional

few dashes Worcestershire sauce, optional

Method

Lightly rinse the tomatoes and roughly chop. Pass through a juicer or blender until the juice is formed, then add sugar to taste and dilute with water, if using. Place a few ice cubes in tall glasses and pour over the tomato juice. Add a twist of lemon and Worcestershire sauce if using and serve.

Alternative Add a little Tabasco sauce in place of the Worcestershire sauce, along with some fresh basil leaves and 2–4 garlic cloves. Or try a selection of fresh herbs: thyme, parsley, rosemary or coriander.

Beetroot and Orange Juice

Beetroot is a vegetable often overlooked, which is a great shame. Even more of a shame is that the leaves of the plant are nearly always thrown away – beetroot leaves provide an excellent source of calcium, iron and beta–carotone.

Ingredients

1 whole raw beetroot complete with leafy
    tops if possible
3 large oranges
3–4 tbsp mineral water to blend, optional
small piece fresh root ginger
chilled mineral water to dilute, optional

Method

Discard the root from the beetroot. Peel the beetroot as thinly as possible, cut into chunks and reserve. Wash the beetroot leaves thoroughly and chop. Peel the oranges, discarding the bitter white pith and divide into segments. Peel the root ginger and chop. Pass through a juicer or blender (adding a little water if blending) until the juice is formed. Pour into glasses and serve diluted with water if liked.

Alternative Omit the ginger and replace with five trimmed and chopped spring onions and a few dashes of Worcestershire or Tabasco sauce for a more spicy flavour.

Cucumber, Apple and Mint Juice

As a member of the squash family, cucumber is naturally a juicy vegetable. When sprinkled lightly with a little freshly ground salt, a cucumber will becomes even juicer. There are two main varieties of cucumber available: ridge, which are short and have little prickles down the sides of the skin, or the traditional smooth–skinned hothouse variety. Both will work well here.

Ingredients

2 ridge or 1 hothouse cucumber

freshly ground salt to sprinkle, optional

2 Granny Smith apples

2 tbsp orange juice

chilled mineral water to dilute, optional

few fresh sprigs of mint

Method

Cut off and reserve a few thin slices of cucumber. Peel the remainder then cut into thick slices and place in a colander and add a twist or two of freshly ground sea salt. Leave for 5–10 minutes. Quarter the apples and discard the cores, then chop. Pass all the ingredients through a juicer or blender until the juice is formed. Pour the juice into glasses, dilute with water if using and decorate with the reserved cucumber slices.

Alternative Simply place the peeled, chopped cucumber into a smoothie machine or blender with the mint and whizz for 2 minutes. Dilute with chilled water.

Pepper Medley

Bell peppers are now as common to us as tomatoes, celery or onions and are readily available in red, yellow, orange or green. Having a sweet flavour they combine well with most ingredients and are perhaps one of our most versatile vegetables.

Ingredients

1 red pepper
1 yellow pepper
1 orange pepper
1 jalapeno chilli, deseeded
1 large orange
few fresh parsley leaves
chilled mineral water to dilute, optional
ice cubes to serve, optional

Method

Cut all the peppers into quarters and discard the seeds and inner membrane then chop roughly. Chop up the chilli. Peel the orange, discarding the bitter white pith, and divide into segments. Pass all the ingredients through a juicer or blender until the juice is formed then dilute with the water, if using. Pour into glasses and add ice cubes before serving, if desired.

Alternative Omit the chilli pepper and use basil in place of the parsley. Whizz the peppers with a little iced water to form a juice. Pour into glasses and dilute with iced water if liked.

Tomato and Celeriac Juice

Look for plump, juicy tomatoes when juicing, as under-ripe tomatoes will not give a satisfactory result – very little juice with a tart flavour. However, do not be tempted to use badly damaged or over-ripe tomatoes, as although the yield will be good the flavour could be seriously impaired.

Ingredients

300 g/10 oz fresh tomatoes

1/2 celeriac, about 300 g/10 oz in weight

4 spring onions, trimmed

chilled mineral water to dilute, optional

2 celery stalks to serve

ice cubes to serve

Method

Lightly rinse the tomatoes then roughly chop. Peel the celeriac and cut into small chunks. Cut the spring onions into small lengths. Pass all the vegetables through a juicer or blender until the juice is formed. Dilute with the water if using. Pour into glasses add a celery stick to each for stirring, along with ice cubes, then serve.

Alternative Add a few dashes of sweet chilli or Tabasco sauce after juicing.

Watercress, Tomato and Leek Juice

Watercress's clean peppery taste combines well with juicy tomatoes and leeks. It is recommended that young, tender leeks are used to give the best results.

Ingredients

100 g/4 oz watercress
225 g/8 oz fresh, ripe tomatoes
100 g/4 oz tender leeks
1 medium orange
 chilled mineral water to dilute, optional

Method

Lightly rinse the watercress and reserve. Rinse the tomatoes, chop and add to the watercress. Trim the leeks, chop roughly and wash thoroughly in cold water. Drain. Peel the orange, discarding the bitter white pith, and divide into segments. Pass through a juicer or blender until the juice is formed, then pour into glasses and dilute with the water if using. Serve.

Alternative Replace the watercress with rocket, sorrel or spinach.
Make sure that they are all thoroughly washed and shake vigorously before using.

Celery, Cucumber and Kiwi Fruit

This cool, green juice is perfect for any time of the day but most especially as a breakfast wake-up call. To get the maximum effect, do ensure that you serve it chilled.

Ingredients

4 celery stalks

1 long hothouse cucumber

2 green kiwi fruits

chilled mineral water to dilute, optional

ice cubes to serve

Method

Trim the celery, removing the stringy threads and chop roughly. Peel the cucumber and discard the seeds, then chop roughly. Scoop out the flesh from the kiwi fruits. Pass all the vegetables through a juicer or blender until the juice is formed, then dilute with the water if using. Pour into glasses, add the ice cubes and serve.

Alternative Replace the kiwi fruits with the flesh from one small melon, discarding the skin and seeds.

Broccoli with Carrot and Orange

Broccoli is one of the best green vegetables that you can eat, and eating any vegetable or fruit raw ensures that none of the valuable nutrients are lost. Wash it well but do not leave soaking in water, otherwise all the nutrients will leach out.

Ingredients

300 g/10 oz broccoli florets
225 g/8 oz carrots
2 large oranges
chilled mineral water to dilute, optional
ice cubes to serve

Method

Cut the broccoli into florets, wash and shake off any excess water. Peel the carrots and cut into even-sized chunks. Peel the oranges, discarding the bitter white pith, and divide into segments. Pass all the ingredients through a juicer or blender until the juice is formed. Dilute with the water if using. Pour into glasses, add ice cubes and serve.

Alternative Replace the broccoli with cauliflower or purple sprouting broccoli, discarding any tough stems.

Tomato, Avocado and Spring Onion

This juice would make a perfect non–alcoholic cocktail. Serve with some Worcestershire or Tabasco sauce and a twist of lime for a refreshing start to any evening.

Ingredients
350 g/12 oz fresh tomatoes

1 ripe avocado

3 tbsp lime juice

4 spring onions

chilled mineral water to dilute

Worcestershire or Tabasco sauce to serve

lime twists to serve

Method
Rinse the tomatoes and chop roughly. Peel the avocado, discard the stone, chop into chunks and toss in the lime juice. Trim the spring onions and chop, then add to the tomatoes and avocado. Pass all the ingredients through a juicer or blender until the juice is formed. Dilute with the water. Pour into glasses and serve with Worcestershire or Tabasco sauce and lime twists.

Alternative Add a small amount of chilli to the ingredients before blending.
Take care not to add too much – more can always be added if it is not spicy enough for your taste.

Tasty Treats

This chapter borders on the indulgent, featuring smoothies that are rich and creamy with the addition of ice cream, yogurt, coconut milk, chocolate and other delicious ingredients. Whether or not you are following a diet or simply being careful in what you eat, we all need to spoil ourselves every now and again. An occasional treat is good for anyone, giving a great feeling of well-being.

When shopping, look for good-quality ingredients. Choose chocolate with a high cocoa butter content and ice cream that is made from eggs and cream – after all, you are not going to eat these every day. If you would prefer a slightly thinner, less rich drink, simply add a little crushed ice.

You'll be spoilt for choice in this chapter: try a Banana Latte – a coffee and banana smoothie topped with crème fraîche, a Chocolate and Raspberry Shake crammed full of fresh, plump raspberries and a scoop of chocolate ice cream, or Apricot Nectar – a smoothie fit for the gods.

Banana Latte

This smooth, delicious drink may sound a little indulgent but it actually is not too over the top. Use freshly brewed coffee made from fresh ground coffee beans rather than instant coffee.

Ingredients

150 ml/¹/₄ pint whole or semi-skimmed milk

300 ml/¹/₂ pint freshly brewed coffee

2 medium, ripe bananas

4–6 ice cubes

2 tbsp half fat crème fraîche, to serve

¹/₂ tsp grated chocolate, to decorate

Method

Blend the milk and coffee together and reserve. Peel the bananas and cut into chunks. Place all the ingredients to be blended in a smoothie machine or blender. If using a smoothie machine, blend on mix for 15 seconds and then on smooth for 30 seconds. In a blender, blend for 1–2 minutes. Place the ice cubes in glasses, pour over the coffee, top with the crème fraîche and sprinkle with the grated chocolate.

Alternative Replace the grated chocolate with a little grated cinnamon and if feeling really indulgent, use whipped cream in place of the crème fraîche.

Apple and Peach Smoothie

When making this smoothie, do ensure that the peaches are ripe – if not, the flavour will be slightly impaired. Try using peach flavoured yogurt for a greater depth of flavour.

Ingredients

2 red apples such as Gala
2 tbsp orange juice
2 ripe peaches
150 ml/¹/₄ pint low fat natural yogurt
ice cubes, to serve

Method

Cut the apples into quarters and discard the core. Chop, then pour the orange juice over them and reserve. Peel the peaches if preferred, cut in half and discard the stones. Place all the ingredients to be blended in a smoothie machine or blender. If using a smoothie machine, blend on mix for 15 seconds and then on smooth for 30 seconds. In a blender, blend for 1–2 minutes. then pour into glasses, add ice cubes and serve.

Alternative If liked, add 1–2 drops of almond essence and replace the yogurt with orange juice. You could also top the smoothies with a spoonful of yogurt.

Berry Smoothie

Choose from a selection of summer berries, such as strawberries, blueberries, raspberries or blackberries. Do ensure that they are in peak condition, perfectly ripe and fresh.

Ingredients

450 g/1 lb mixed summer berries
1 large ripe banana, peeled
6 tbsp frozen strawberry yogurt
extra berries, to decorate

Method

Clean the fruits, cutting any larger fruits in half or quarters. Place all the ingredients to be blended in a smoothie machine or blender. If using a smoothie machine, blend on mix for 15 seconds and then on smooth for 30 seconds. In a blender, blend for 1–2 minutes. Pour into tall glasses, decorate the glasses with the berries and serve immediately

Alternative Add six ice cubes to the berries and banana before blending and once the ice is crushed, pour into tall glasses and top with a scoop of vanilla ice cream.

Apricot and Apple Smoothie

Apricots are similar to plums in size, shape and texture. They are seasonal and, unlike many of our fruits, not available all year round. Take advantage of apricots when they are in season and enjoy this refreshing drink.

Ingredients

2 Golden Delicious apples

6 ripe apricots

1 ripe banana, peeled and chopped

1–2 tsp clear honey, or to taste

200 ml/7 fl oz natural yogurt

1–2 drops almond essence, optional

ice cubes, to serve

Method

Cut the apples into quarters and discard the cores. Lightly rinse the apricots, cut in half and discard the stones. Add to the apples together with the banana. Place all the ingredients to be blended in a smoothie machine or blender. If using a smoothie machine, blend on mix for 15 seconds and then on smooth for 30 seconds. In a blender, blend for 1–2 minutes before pouring into glasses, adding ice cubes and serving.

Alternative Omit the apples and replace with 150 ml/$^1/_4$ pint unsweetened apple juice. Use an extra chopped banana.

Chocolate and Raspberry Shake

Every now and again a special treat is called for. A real chocoholic as well as raspberries being one of my favourite fruits, this is a combination that I simply cannot resist.

Ingredients

350 g/12 oz fresh raspberries

3 tbsp orange juice

300 ml/^{1}/$_2$ pint whole or semi–skimmed milk

2 tbsp grated plain dark chocolate

few ice cubes

2 scoops chocolate or vanilla ice cream

Method

Lightly rinse the raspberries. Place the orange juice and milk with the raspberries and 1 ^{1}/$_2$ tablespoons of the grated chocolate in a smoothie machine or blender. If using a smoothie machine, blend on mix for 15 seconds and then on smooth for 30 seconds. In a blender, blend for 1–2 minutes then pour into glasses, add ice cubes, top with the ice cream and sprinkle with the remaining grated chocolate.

Alternative If you prepare this drink in a blender, you may prefer to pass it through a fine nylon sieve to remove the raspberry seeds. Make the smoothie more healthy by replacing the milk with orange juice and using spoonfuls of low fat natural yogurt on top in place of the ice cream.

Tropical Delight

You can vary the fruits used in this smoothie according to taste and availability.
Ensure that the fruits are at their best – ripe and full of flavour and aroma.

Ingredients

1 large ripe mango
1 large ripe papaya
2 ripe bananas. peeled and cut into chunks
juice of $^1/_2$ lime
2–3 tsp clear honey
300 ml/$^1/_2$ pint coconut milk
ice cubes, to serve

Method

Peel the mango and papaya and discard the stone and seeds. Chop the fruits into large chunks and pour over the lime juice, then place all the ingredients to be blended in a smoothie machine or blender. If using a smoothie machine, blend on mix for 15 seconds and then on smooth for 30 seconds. In a blender, blend for 1–2 minutes. Place some ice cubes into tall glasses and add the prepared drink. Serve immediately.

Alternative Replace the coconut milk with Greek yogurt and spinkle the top with a little ground cinnamon.

Banana and Chocolate Shake

When buying chocolate, buy the best that you can afford. Look for chocolate with the highest cocoa butter content – 60 per cent or higher is good. This means the flavour is better and more intense and you will be able to use less than if using the cheaper bars.

Ingredients

3 ripe bananas

40 g/1¹/₂ oz plain dark chocolate, grated

450 ml/³/₄ pint chilled whole or semi–skimmed milk

2 scoops of good quality vanilla or chocolate ice cream

Method

Peel the bananas and cut into chunks. Place the banana, the chocolate and the milk in a smoothie machine or blender. If using a smoothie machine, blend on mix for 15 seconds and then on smooth for 30 seconds. In a blender, blend for 1–2 minutes. Pour into glasses and top with scoops of ice cream.

Alternative Use two bananas and add 100 g/4 oz fresh raspberries to the fruits before blending.

Honeyed Figs with Yogurt

There are three main varieties of fig: green, purple and red, all of which are grown mainly in the Mediterranean countries. They are at their best when fresh and ripe, bursting with flavour and aroma. You can also buy them dried or semi-dried, but these would need a little cooking in some orange juice before using to make this smoothie.

Ingredients

4–6 fresh ripe figs, depending on size

300 ml/$^1/_2$ pint Greek yogurt

2–3 tsp clear honey

1 tbsp grated orange rind

4–6 ice cubes

Method

Cut the figs in half and scoop out their flesh and place all the ingredients to be blended in a smoothie machine or blender. If using a smoothie machine, blend on mix for 15 seconds and then on smooth for 30 seconds. In a blender, blend for 1–2 minutes, then pour into glasses and serve immediately.

Alternative If fresh figs are not available, gently poach 100 g/4 oz chopped dried figs in 150 ml/$^1/_4$ pint of orange juice for 10 minutes or until very soft, then use as per the fresh figs.

Passion Fruit and Guava Special

Use passion fruit juice if fresh fruits are not available or you cannot wait for the fruits to ripen. Don't be tempted to use under-ripe fruits for this, as the flavours will be seriously impaired.

Ingredients

2 ripe passion fruits

2 ripe guavas

2 Golden Delicious apples

6 scoops good quality vanilla ice cream

Method

Scoop the flesh and seeds from the passion fruits and if liked, sieve to remove the seeds. Discard the seeds from the guavas. Cut the apples into quarters and discard the cores and cut into wedges. Reserve two scoops of the ice cream, placing all the other ingredients in a smoothie machine or blender. If using a smoothie machine, blend on mix for 15 seconds and then on smooth for 30 seconds. In a blender, blend for 1–2 minutes. Pour into glasses, top with the remaining ice cream and serve.

Alternative Use one large, ripe orange in place of the apples, discarding the peel and bitter white pithbefore chopping into chunks.

Pineapple and Raspberry Smoothie

This smoothie can be enjoyed all year round as both fruits are now readily available. If you are fortunate enough to have your own fruit garden and grow raspberries, this is a great recipe for using the fruits that are not perfect to look at but are ripe and bursting with the summer sun.

Ingredients

1 medium, ripe pineapple

225 g/8 oz fresh raspberries

150 ml/$^1/_4$ pint orange juice

6 ice cubes

1 tbsp lightly whipped cream, to serve

1–2 tsp grated plain dark chocolate, to decorate

Method

Discard the plume and skin from the pineapple and cut lengthways into quarters. Discard the hard central core and cut the flesh into chunks. Place all the ingredients to be blended in a smoothie machine or blender. If using a smoothie machine, blend on mix for 15 seconds and then on smooth for 30 seconds. In a blender, blend for 1–2 minutes. Pour into glasses and top with the cream. Sprinkle with the grated chocolate and serve immediately.

Alternative Omit the orange juice and replace with coconut milk and sprinkle with a little toasted desiccated coconut.

Apricot Nectar

When you are feeling like giving yourself an extra-special treat or just need to indulge, then this smoothie is perfect for you. Make and enjoy at leisure.

Ingredients

6 fresh, ripe apricots
6 scoops good quality vanilla ice cream
300 ml/¹/₂ pint orange juice
1 tsp toasted flaked almonds, to serve

Method

Lightly rinse the apricots, cut in half and discard the stones. Reserve two scoops of the ice cream. Place all the other ingredients to be blended in a smoothie machine or blender. If using a smoothie machine, blend on mix for 15 seconds and then on smooth for 30 seconds. In a blender, blend for 1–2 minutes. Pour into glasses, top with the remaining ice cream, sprinkle with the flaked almonds and serve.

Alternative Use peaches or nectarines in place of the apricots and add 1–2 drops of almond essence.

Mango and Blackberry Crush

Whenever possible it is best to use fresh fruits when making smoothies, but in some instances canned or frozen fruits are fine. This recipe works well with either – if fresh ripe mangos are not available, then use drained, canned mangos.

Ingredients

2 fresh, ripe mangos or 400 g can mango
150 g/5 oz fresh blackberries
300 ml/¹/₂ pint apple and elderflower juice
2 scoops vanilla ice cream, to serve
few extra blackberries, to decorate

Method

If using fresh mangos, peel, cut the flesh away from the stone, chop and reserve. If using canned mangos, drain. Place all the ingredients to be blended in a smoothie machine or blender. If using a smoothie machine, blend on mix for 15 seconds and then on smooth for 30 seconds. In a blender, blend for 1–2 minutes. Pour into glasses, top with a scoop of ice cream and decorate with the extra blackberries before serving.

Alternative Replace the blackberries with blueberries and if liked, add 1–2 teaspoons of finely grated orange rind.

Cool Raspberry Soda

If you are fortunate enough to have a pick–your–own fruit farm near you, look for one of the many berries that are available in small outlets. Loganberries, boysenberries or tayberries are the ones you are most likely to find, and they would make a delicious substitution for the raspberries in this recipe.

Ingredients
450 g/1 lb fresh raspberries
1–2 tsp clear honey
4 tbsp orange juice
6 ice cubes
2 scoops raspberry ripple ice cream, to serve
soda water, to serve

Method
Hull and clean the raspberries, if necessary, and place all the ingredients to be blended in a smoothie machine or blender. If using a smoothie machine, blend on mix for 15 seconds and then on smooth for 30 seconds. In a blender, blend for 1–2 minutes. Pour into glasses, top with a scoop of ice cream and soda water and serve immediately.

Alternative Replace the raspberries with fresh strawberries, cutting them in half if large, and use strawberry ice cream.

Choc and Orange 99

Chocolate can be an indulgence, but it also contains natural amphetamines which stimulate the central nervous system and give a feeling of well–being.

Ingredients

300 ml/¹/₂ pint whole or semi–skimmed milk

25 g/1 oz good quality dark chocolate, grated

2 tsp finely grated orange rind

6 ice cubes

2 scoops good quality vanilla or chocolate ice cream, to serve

1–2 tbsp whipped cream, to serve

chocolate flake, to serve

Method

Place all the ingredients, including the chocolate and ice cubes, in a smoothie machine or blender. If using a smoothie machine, blend on mix for 15 seconds and then on smooth for 30 seconds. In a blender, blend for 1–2 minutes. Pour into glasses, top with the ice cream, whipped cream and chocolate flake and serve.

Alternative Replace the orange rind with the segmented flesh from one large orange and top with spoonfuls of Greek yogurt or crème fraîche.

Banana with Ginger Cream

There are many forms of ginger available, ranging from fresh root ginger and ground ginger to stem and crystallized ginger, which are far sweeter. Use whichever you prefer when making the cream for this recipe.

Ingredients

2 large, ripe bananas

2 large oranges

150 ml/^{1}/$_4$ pint coconut milk

6 ice cubes

2 tbsp whipped double cream, to serve

1 tsp ginger (either grated fresh root, or ground) to decorate

1 tsp crystallized ginger, chopped

Method

Peel the bananas and cut into chunks. Peel the orange, discarding the bitter white pith, and divide into the segments. Place all the ingredients to be blended, including the ice cubes, in a smoothie machine or blender. If using a smoothie machine, blend on mix for 15 seconds and then on smooth for 30 seconds. In a blender, blend for 1–2 minutes. Mix the cream and ginger together and stir half into the banana drink. Pour into glasses, top with the remaining cream, sprinkle with the chopped crystallized ginger and serve.

Alternative Replace one of the bananas with 175 g/6 oz peeled and stoned lychees.

Apricot and Passion Fruit Lassi

Apricots originate from China but are now widely available when in season. This recipe blends lush, fresh apricots with lychees, aromatic passion fruits and natural yogurt, resulting in an absolutely fabulous drink.

Ingredients

6 ripe apricots
2 ripe passion fruits
100 g/4 oz lychees
150 ml/¼ pint natural yogurt
150 ml/¼ pint apple juice
6 ice cubes

Method

Lightly rinse the apricots and cut in half, discarding the stones. Cut the passion fruits in half and scoop out the seeds and flesh. Sieve the flesh if preferred. Peel and stone the lychees, then place all the ingredients (including the ice cubes) in a smoothie machine or blender. If using a smoothie machine, blend on mix for 15 seconds and then on smooth for 30 seconds. In a blender, blend for 1–2 minutes. Pour into glasses and serve immediately.

Alternative Replace the lychees with one ripe, peeled banana.
If liked, use Greek yogurt in place of the natural yogurt.

Mango Lassi

Lassi is a very popular drink and originated in India, providing a cool, refreshing drink to enjoy in hot weather or after spicy food. It is drunk at any time of the day, often throughout a meal or as a mid–morning snack.

Ingredients

2 ripe mangos
250 ml/8 fl oz natural yogurt
150 ml/¼ pint semi–skimmed milk
1–2 tsp clear honey, or to taste
6 ice cubes
1 mint sprig, optional

Method

Peel the mango and cut the flesh away from the stone. Cut into chunks and place all the ingredients in a smoothie machine or blender. If using a smoothie machine, blend on mix for 15 seconds and then on smooth for 30 seconds. In a blender, blend for 1–2 minutes. Pour into glasses and serve.

Alternative Replace the mango with any of the following fruits: strawberries, raspberries, bananas or peaches.

Papaya and Ginger Cup

This is an indulgent drink that will not only make you feel good due to its delicious taste, but will also keep your stomach healthy thanks to the addition of ginger and yogurt.

Ingredients

2 ripe papayas, peeled and seeded
150 ml/¼ pint freshly squeezed orange juice
1 tsp finely grated orange rind
small piece root ginger, peeled and grated
100 g/4 oz lychees, peeled and stoned
300 ml/½ pint natural yogurt
6 ice cubes
2 sprigs fresh mint, to decorate

Method

Place all the ingredients to be blended, including the ice cubes, in a smoothie machine or blender. If using a smoothie machine, blend on mix for 15 seconds and then on smooth for 30 seconds. In a blender, blend for 1–2 minutes. Pour into glasses and serve decorated with a mint sprig.

Alternative Replace the orange juice with pineapple juice and decorate the glasses with a wedge of pineapple.

Iced Chocolate and Peppermint Latte

Chocolate and peppermint are a fantastic combination, so this latte will appeal to all ages. It is also incredibly quick to prepare.

Ingredients

600 ml/1 pint whole or semi–skimmed milk

40 g/1¹/₂ oz good quality dark or milk chocolate, grated

1–2 drops peppermint essence

4–6 ice cubes

2 scoops vanilla ice cream, to serve

2–4 chocolate peppermint thins to decorate

Method

Place all the ingredients to be blended (including the ice cubes) in a smoothie machine or blender. If using a smoothie machine, blend on mix for 15 seconds and then on smooth for 30 seconds. In a blender, blend for 1–2 minutes. Pour into tall glasses. Top with the ice cream and decorate with the chocolate peppermint thins before serving.

Alternative Replace the vanilla ice cream with chocolate ice cream or spoonfuls of whipped cream.

Honeyed Banana Soda

When using honey in cooking, whether it is in drinks, desserts or savoury dishes, always use clear honey unless the recipe states otherwise. It is far easier to pour and blends quickly with the other ingredients.

Ingredients

2 large, ripe bananas

2 tbsp freshly squeezed orange juice

1 tbsp clear honey

300 ml/^{1}/$_2$ pint coconut milk

2 ice cubes

^{1}/$_2$ tsp freshly grated nutmeg

soda water, to serve

Method

Peel and chop the bananas and pour the orange juice over them. Place all the ingredients except the soda water in a smoothie machine or blender. If using a smoothie machine, blend on mix for 15 seconds and then on smooth for 30 seconds. In a blender, blend for 1–2 minutes. Pour into glasses, add a little soda water to dilute and serve.

Alternative Replace the coconut milk with natural yogurt and use ground cinnamon in place of the nutmeg. Add a long cinnamon stick for stirring.

Raspberry Pavlova

This recipe is based on the very popular dessert of the same name and provides a delicious indulgence, something we all need occasionally. Try it and see.

Ingredients

225 g/8 oz fresh or thawed frozen raspberries

150 ml/¼ pint whole or semi–skimmed milk

2 scoops vanilla ice cream

2 tbsp lightly whipped cream, to serve

2–4 tiny meringues, to serve

2 chocolate–filled rolled wafer biscuits, to serve

Method

Place the raspberries, milk and ice cream in a smoothie machine or blender. If using a smoothie machine, blend on mix for 15 seconds and then on smooth for 30 seconds. In a blender, blend for 1–2 minutes. Pour into glasses, top with the whipped cream and crumble over the meringues. Serve immediately with the biscuits.

Alternative Use other fruits in place of the raspberries – try fresh, ripe peaches, nectarines, strawberries or blueberries.

Lemon Meringue Shake

When using the rind from citrus fruits, wherever possible use organic fruits as these have not been sprayed with chemicals. Organic or not, it is still important that the fruits are thoroughly washed before using the rind.

Ingredients

1 tbsp finely grated lemon rind

50 ml/2 fl oz freshly squeezed lemon juice

1–2 tbsp clear honey, or to taste

300 ml/¹/₂ pint whole or semi–skimmed milk

4 scoops lemon sorbet

2 tbsp lightly whipped cream, to serve

2 small meringues, to decorate

Method

Place the lemon rind and juice in a smoothie machine or blender and add the honey, milk and sorbet. Whizz for 45 seconds to 1 minute or until smooth. Pour into glasses and top with the cream. Crumble the meringues and sprinkle over the top, then serve.

Alternative Replace the lemon with orange or lime or even all three.
Raspberries would also work well, especially if combined with raspberry sorbet.

Peanut Butter Smoothie

Peanut butter is one of those ingredients that is either loved or hated. If you love it, then this smoothie is for you. I would recommend that you use the smooth rather than the crunchy variety, but of course the choice is yours.

Ingredients

2 tbsp smooth peanut butter

1 large, ripe banana

2 tbsp freshly squeezed orange juice

150 ml/¹/₄ pint whole or semi-skimmed milk

150 ml/¹/₄ pint natural yogurt

4 ice cubes

2 tbsp crème fraîche, to serve

2 tsp good quality drinking chocolate, to decorate

Method

Place all the ingredients to be blended, including the ice cubes, in a smoothie machine or blender. If using a smoothie machine, blend on mix for 15 seconds and then on smooth for 30 seconds. In a blender, blend for 1–2 minutes. Pour into glasses and top with a spoonful of crème fraîche and a little drinking chocolate.

Alternative Make the smoothie a little spicy and add a few splashes of either sweet chilli sauce or Tabasco sauce

Dreamy Coffee and Chocolate Shake

There are many different coffees now readily available, ranging from the very strong Turkish blends, the smooth Brazilian taste, the full-bodied flavour that is Colombian coffee to the subtle mellow flavour of Java coffee. Choose your favourite blend to enjoy this smoothie at its best.

Ingredients

200 ml/7 fl oz freshly brewed coffee

200 ml/7 fl oz whole or semi-skimmed milk

50 g/2 oz good quality plain dark chocolate, grated

$^1/_2$ tsp ground cinnamon

2 small scoops vanilla ice cream

2 small scoops chocolate ice cream

2 long cinnamon sticks

Method

Place all the ingredients to be blended, including a scoop of each ice cream, in a smoothie machine or blender. If using a smoothie machine, blend on mix for 15 seconds and then on smooth for 30 seconds. In a blender, blend for 1–2 minutes. Pour into glasses and top with the remaining scoops of vanilla and chocolate ice cream. Add the cinnamon sticks and serve.

Alternative Replace the ice cream with spoonfuls of whipped cream.

Summer Special

Blackcurrants and redcurrants are lush, plump fruits full of the summer sun, especially redcurrants with their bright red skins that evoke long, lazy days. Whitecurrants, if you can find them, also burst with flavour. Try this recipe with all three currants if available, or with just one or two of them.

Ingredients

350 g/12 oz fresh currants, black, red and white
   if available
2–3 tbsp clear honey
200 ml/7 fl oz whole or semi-skimmed milk
150 ml/^{1}/$_4$ pint natural yogurt
2 scoops vanilla ice cream, to serve
extra redcurrants to decorate, optional

Method

String the currants, rinse and reserve. Place in a smoothie machine or blender with the honey, milk and yogurt. Whizz for 45 seconds to 1 minute. In a blender, blend for 1–2 minutes and then pass through a fine nylon sieve to remove the pips. Pour into glasses. Add the ice cream to each glass and decorate with the redcurrants if using. Serve.

Alternative If no fresh currants are available, use blackcurrant juice or a combination of juices containing blackcurrant. Omit the honey and decorate with a little grated chocolate.

Orange Flip

Take care when selecting the eggs for this recipe. Use eggs that are as fresh as possible and before use, store either in their box or in the egg compartment of the fridge. Allow to come to room temperure for 30 minutes before using. If you are pregnant or have recently recovered from illness, it is recommended that you do not make this drink.

Ingredients

2 medium eggs

2–3 tsp clear honey

300 ml/$^1/_2$ pint freshly squeezed orange juice

2 tbsp freshly squeezed lemon juice

6 ice cubes

Method

Place all the ingredients in a smoothie machine or blender. If using a smoothie machine, blend on mix for 15 seconds and then on smooth for 30 seconds. In a blender, blend for 1–2 minutes. Pour into glasses and serve immediately.

Alternative Replace the orange juice with 300 ml/$^1/_2$ pint blackcurrant juice and top with a spoonful of whipped cream.

Pineapple Smoothie

For this smoothie you can use either fresh pineapple or pineapple juice: the choice is yours, depending on whether you prefer a smooth drink or if you like the pieces of fruit.

Ingredients

1 medium, ripe pineapple

2 ripe passion fruits, flesh and seeds scooped out

1 large, ripe banana, peeled and cut into chunks

300 ml/¹/₂ pint natural yogurt

2–3 tsp clear honey

4 ice cubes

2 scoops vanilla ice cream, to serve

1 tsp grated milk chocolate, to decorate

Method

Prepare the pineapple, discarding the plume, skin and hard central core and cut into chunks. Sieve the passion fruit if a smooth texture is preferred. Place all the ingredients to be blended, including the ice cubes, in a smoothie machine or blender. If using a smoothie machine, blend on mix for 15 seconds and then on smooth for 30 seconds. In a blender, blend for 1–2 minutes. Pour into glasses, top with the ice cream and sprinkle with the grated chocolate before serving.

Alternative Replace the passion fruit with strawberries and use strawberry flavoured yogurt.

Strawberry Delight

If possible, use locally grown strawberries as they usually have more flavour than fruit that has been packaged in a supermarket. Try to avoid keeping strawberries in the fridge, but if you have to, remove them at least 30 minutes before using.

Ingredients

300 g/10 oz fresh, ripe strawberries
few shakes of freshly ground black pepper
150 ml/¹/₄ pint strawberry yogurt
150 ml/¹/₄ pint natural yogurt
2 scoops vanilla ice cream
2 tbsp whipped cream, to serve
strawberry fans to decorate, optional

Method

Hull then lightly rinse the strawberries and if large, cut in half. Place all the ingredients to be blended, including the scoops of ice cream, in a smoothie machine or blender. If using a smoothie machine, blend on mix for 15 seconds and then on smooth for 30 seconds. In a blender, blend for 1–2 minutes. Pour into glasses and top with the cream. Decorate each with a strawberry fan if using.

Alternative Using freshly ground black pepper with strawberries helps to bring out the flavour.
A few drops of balsamic vinegar also has the same effect. If preferred, use a little clear honey.

Apple Crumble Smoothie

Replace a favourite pudding with a smoothie that is simple to prepare, ready in minutes and tastes fantastic. Other fruits can be used instead of apple, much as you can substitute the fruits in a crumble.

Ingredients

3 Gala eating apples (or any other sweet and juicy apples)

2 tsp finely grated orange rind

75 ml/3 fl oz apple juice

300 ml/$^1/_2$ pint natural yogurt

150 ml/$^1/_4$ pint freshly made custard

2 scoops vanilla ice cream, to serve

2 digestive biscuits, to serve

1 tbsp toasted, crushed flaked almonds, to decorate

Method

Cut the apples into quarters and discard the cores. Chop into chunks and place all the ingredients to be blended in a smoothie machine or blender. If using a smoothie machine, blend on mix for 15 seconds and then on smooth for 30 seconds. In a blender, blend for 1–2 minutes. Pour into glasses and top with the ice cream. Break the biscuits in half and place in the ice cream, sprinkle with the almonds and serve.

Alternative Replace the digestive biscuits with a crumbled muesli bar.

Cherry Jubilee

Cherries are one of the fruits that are only obtainable seasonally, so when they are around make the most of them. Although it is not possible to buy frozen cherries, they do freeze reasonably well, so when in season buy more than you need and freeze some.

Ingredients

300 g/10 oz fresh, ripe cherries, pitted

75 ml/3 fl oz apple juice

300 ml/^{1}/$_2$ pint cherry flavoured yogurt

6 ice cubes

2 tbsp whipped cream, to serve

extra cherries, to decorate

Method

Place all the ingredients to be blended, including the ice cubes, in a smoothie machine or blender. If using a smoothie machine, blend on mix for 15 seconds and then on smooth for 30 seconds. In a blender, blend for 1–2 minutes. Pour into glasses, top with the cream and decorate with the cherries.

Alternative Replace the cherries with blackberries and decorate with whole blackberries.

Fruit Medley Lassi

If you are looking for a real taste sensation, then this is the drink for you. With a wonderful depth of flavour and aroma, it not only tastes good but with all its vitamin C content will do you good as well.

Ingredients

100 g/4 oz strawberries

100 g/4 oz raspberries

100 g/4 oz blackberries

1 ripe passion fruit, flesh and seeds scooped out

200 ml/7 fl oz coconut milk

4 scoops vanilla ice cream

extra fruits and mint sprigs to decorate, optional

Method

Hull the strawberries and lightly rinse all the berries. Sieve the passion fruit if preferred. Place all the ingredients to be blended, including two scoops of the ice cream, in a smoothie machine or blender. If using a smoothie machine, blend on mix for 15 seconds then on smooth for 30 seconds. In a blender, blend for 1–2 minutes. Pour into glasses, top with the remaining ice cream and decorate with the fruits and mint sprigs if using.

Alternative Omit the ice cream and replace with six ice cubes.
Add two sprigs of fresh mint before blending.

Aromatic Mango Lassi

Aromatic spices are widely available in most supermarkets, so add a touch of the Orient to your smoothie. When buying spices, unless you use them often, buy in small quantities as their aroma and flavour do not last for long. Store them away from the light in airtight containers.

Ingredients

2 large, ripe mangos

4 cardamom pods

1 small piece star anise

2 tsp clear honey

150 ml/^{1}/$_4$ pint apple juice

150 ml/^{1}/$_4$ pint coconut milk

150 ml/^{1}/$_4$ pint natural yogurt

cinnamon stick to stir

Method

Peel the mangos, cut the flesh away from the stones, cut the flesh into chunks and reserve. Crush the cardamom pods and the star anise. Place all the ingredients to be blended in a smoothie machine or blender. If using a smoothie machine, blend on mix for 15 seconds and then on smooth for 30 seconds. In a blender, blend for 1–2 minutes. Pour into glasses and serve with the cinnamon stick to stir.

Alternative Replace the mango with papaya and use orange juice rather than apple.

Detox Drinks

When feeling under the weather, run down and generally not well, a detox diet can work wonders. Within the body there is a network of glands called the lymph system, designed to drain off excess fluid and help rid the body of unwelcome infections. If the lymphatic fluids become infected they can carry the infection to various parts of the body, so it is important to keep these glands healthy. The gall bladder and liver also help in the fight against infections. A detox diet will assist the lymph system in staying healthy as well as helping to purify the blood, promote good circulation and eliminate toxins from the body.

The drinks in this chapter use produce which will help when following a detoxifying diet. These recipes use plenty of vegetables and fruits with herbs and extracts, all of which produce excellent results. Choose Watermelon with Kiwi and Echinacea, excellent for helping the immune system and the lymph glands, or a smoothie containing fresh rosemary, an excellent stimulant for the circulation and also good for the memory. Many of these smoothies are thick and creamy but if preferred, dilute with extra crushed ice. Get smoothing and get healthy!

Breakfast Smoothie

Breakfast is the most important meal, setting you up for the rest of the day. Eating the right food for breakfast will stop you being tempted by those mid–morning snacks. The wheat germ in this recipe is an excellent source of folic acid and vitamin E, which protects cell membranes and prevents the build up of plaque in the arteries. Try this in place of coffee or tea.

Ingredients

1 large banana
300 ml/¹/₂ pint freshly squeezed orange juice
4 ice cubes
1 tbsp wheat germ

Method

Peel the banana and add to the smoothie machine or blender with the other ingredients. If using a smoothie machine, blend on mix for 15 seconds and then on smooth for 45 seconds. In a blender, blend for 1–2 minutes or until smooth. Pour into glasses and serve.

Alternative Replace the orange juice with one peeled and segmented whole orange.

Pick–Me–Up Smoothie

If you feel that you are in need of a good pick–me–up then this smoothie is for you. It contains wheat grass, an antioxidant with many other health benefits. This smoothie is excellent for vegetarians, as it contains all the B group vitamins.

Ingredients

2 eating apples

150 ml/^{1}/$_4$ pint probiotic bio live natural yogurt

300 ml/^{1}/$_2$ pint apple juice

2 rounded tsp wheat grass powder

4 ice cubes

Method

Cut the apples into quarters, core and chop. Place in a smoothie machine or blender with the yogurt, apple juice, wheat grass and ice cubes. If using a smoothie machine, blend on mix for 15 seconds and then on smooth for 45 seconds. In a blender, blend for 1–2 minutes or until smooth. Pour into glasses and serve.

Alternative Replace the apple juice with freshly brewed nettle tea, or if available add a small handful of fresh, rinsed nettles and filtered water, rather than the nettle tea, before blending.

Watermelon and Flax Oil Smoothie

Flax seed is available in capsule form as well as oil, and is a rich source of omega–3 fatty acids. One flax seed capsule will provide the body's daily requirement.

Ingredients

$^1/_2$ small watermelon (about 300 g/10 oz in weight after skin is discarded)

2 large oranges

2 tbsp flax oil

Method

Remove the watermelon skin, discard the seeds and cut into chunks. Peel the oranges, discarding the bitter white pith, then cut into chunks. Place in a smoothie machine or blender and add the flax oil. If using a smoothie machine, blend on mix for 15 seconds and then on smooth for 45 seconds. In a blender, blend for 1–2 minutes or until smooth. Pour into glasses and serve.

Alternative Use honeydew or gallia melon if a watermelon is not available.

Herb Special

It has long been accepted that herbs can have a beneficial effect on the body, and can be used in many cases to both heal and promote general well–being. So when on a detox diet, do not overlook herbs. This drink will help eliminate fluid from the body – dandelions are a strong diuretic and good for detoxing of the blood as well as the liver.

Ingredients

small handful dandelion leaves

small handful lovage leaves

1 hothouse cucumber

300 ml/$^{1}/_{2}$ pint dandelion and burdock drink

6 ice cubes (made using filtered water)

Method

Thoroughly wash all the herbs and pat dry. Place in a smoothie machine or blender. Peel the cucumber and discard the seeds. Cut into chunks and add to the leaves together with the liquid and ice cubes. If using a smoothie machine, blend on mix for 15 seconds and then on smooth for 45 seconds. In a blender, blend for 1–2 minutes or until smooth. Pour into glasses and serve immediately.

Alternative If this is a little bitter for your taste buds, replace the dandelion and burdock with freshly squeezed orange juice and, if still too bitter, a small squeeze of clear honey.

Carrot and Parsley Smoothie

Parsley is a good diuretic, it stimulates the liver and is rich in vitamin C. Try this smoothie if you have overdone the alcohol and have woken up feeling rough. If you are feeling organized, you could collect the ingredients before you go out in the evening and just quickly whizz them together in the morning.

Ingredients

175 g/6 oz carrots, peeled

2 apples, cored

1 hothouse cucumber

150 ml/¹/₄ pint dandelion and burdock drink

few dandelion leaves, rinsed

small handful parsley, rinsed

150 ml/¹/₄ pint probiotic bio–live natural yogurt

Method

Cut the carrots and apples into chunks and place in a smoothie machine or blender. Peel the cucumber and discard the seeds. Chop and place in the machine. Add the dandelion and burdock drink, herbs and leaves with the yogurt. If using a smoothie machine, blend on mix for 15 seconds and then on smooth for 45 seconds. In a blender, blend for 1–2 minutes or until smooth. Pour into glasses and serve.

Alternative Replace the dandelion and burdock with green tea and add some milk thistle and burdock leaves, if available.

Carrot and Oregano Juice

Both oregano and rosemary are excellent for detoxing and stimulating the lymphatic system and circulation

Ingredients

175 g/6 oz carrots
2 celery stalks
100 g/4 oz fresh spinach leaves
2–3 sprigs fresh oregano leaves
1–2 sprigs fresh rosemary
300 ml/$^1/_2$ pint unsweetened apple juice
4 ice cubes

Method

Peel the carrots and cut into chunks. Trim the celery, cut into chunks and place with the carrots in a smoothie machine or blender. Add the herbs with the apple juice and ice cubes. If using a smoothie machine, blend on mix for 15 seconds and then on smooth for 45 seconds. In a blender, blend for 1–2 minutes or until smooth. Pour into glasses and serve.

Alternative Try other herbs such as angelica, lovage, marigold, ginger and dock root.
All help to stimulate the lymphatic system and promote good circulation.

Tomato, Celery and Marigold Smoothie

Both the flower and leaves of the marigold can be eaten, but do make sure that you wash both thoroughly before use. Marigold is good for cleansing the lymphatic system, liver and gall bladder as well as improving circulation.

Ingredients

225 g/8 oz ripe tomatoes

1 eating apple, cored

1 courgette, peeled

few marigold flower heads and leaves

150 ml/¹/₄ pint unsweetened apple juice

4 ice cubes

2 extra marigold flowers, to serve

Method

Cut the tomatoes, apple and courgette into chunks and place in a smoothie machine or blender with the marigold flowers and leaves. Add the apple juice and ice cubes. If using a smoothie machine, blend on mix for 15 seconds and then on smooth for 45 seconds. In a blender, blend for 1–2 minutes or until smooth. Pour into glasses and serve with a marigold flower floating on top, if liked.

Alternative Replace the marigold flowers and leaves with 2–3 sprigs of fresh thyme, also good for improving the circulation.

Watermelon with Kiwi and Echinacea

Echinacea is well known for helping the immune system, but it can also be used to stimulate the lymph glands, help the circulation and to purify the blood.

Ingredients

1 large wedge watermelon (about $^1/_2$ of a large fruit)

3 kiwi fruits

few drops echinacea tincture

1–2 tsp finely grated orange rind

4 ice cubes

Method

Discard the skin and seeds form the watermelon, cut the flesh into chunks and place in a smoothie machine or blender. Scoop the flesh from the kiwi fruits into the machine and add the echinacea, orange rind and ice cubes. If using a smoothie machine, blend on mix for 15 seconds and then on smooth for 45 seconds. In a blender, blend for 1–2 minutes or until smooth. Pour into glasses and serve.

Alternative Add the peeled and segmented flesh from one large orange and add a small handful of chives to help purify the blood.

95

Banana with Strawberries and Angelica

When using angelica, use washed and dried fresh leaves, seeds or stem, not the candied variety. Angelica tends to be overlooked these days and relegated to the decoration of cakes and desserts. However if you are lucky enough to have a plant, use the fresh leaves and stems in this delicious drink – good for stimulating the circulation and as a digestive and expectorant.

Ingredients

2 ripe bananas

225 g/8 oz strawberries

small piece fresh angelica stem or a few seeds and
    a couple of leaves

150 ml/¹/₄ pint green tea

1 tbsp rolled oats

4 ice cubes

Method

Peel and chop the bananas and cut the strawberries in half if large. Place in a smoothie machine or blender with the chopped angelica, tea, oats and ice cubes. If using a smoothie machine, blend on mix for 15 seconds and then on smooth for 45 seconds. In a blender, blend for 1–2 minutes or until smooth. Pour into glasses and serve.

Alternative Omit the bananas and use twice the amount of strawberries,
adding an extra tablespoon of rolled oats.

Fennel and Orange with Aloe Vera

Aloe vera has been used throughout the ages to treat infections, allergies and inflammation. It has also been used in treatment for ME, candida and detoxification. It can be used both orally, as here, and applied to the skin.

Ingredients

1 large Florence fennel bulb

2 large oranges, peeled and segmented

1 ridge or $1/2$ hothouse cucumber

25 ml/1 fl oz aloe vera juice

1–2 shakes cayenne pepper

6 ice cubes

Method

Thoroughly wash the fennel and cut into chunks. Place in a smoothie machine or blender together with the peeled and segmented oranges. Peel the cucumber, discard the seeds then chop. Add to the machine with the aloe vera, cayenne pepper and ice cubes. If using a smoothie machine, blend on mix for 15 seconds and then on smooth for 45 seconds. In a blender, blend for 1–2 minutes or until smooth. Pour into glasses and serve.

Alternative Replace the fennel bulb with a head of celery, trimming the stalks and washing thoroughly before use. Reserve the smaller celery stalks with leaves and use to stir the drink.

Orange with Algae

Algae is reputed to be very beneficial in the detoxification of the body. It comes either from freshwater lakes or it is farmed, and comes in both powder and tablet form. Use the powder here.

Ingredients

2 large oranges

3 tbsp sprouted broccoli seeds

$\frac{1}{2}$ tsp algae powder

6 ice cubes

Method

Peel the oranges, discarding the bitter white pith, and divide into segments. Place in a smoothie machine or blender with the sprouted seeds, algae powder and ice cubes. If using a smoothie machine, blend on mix for 15 seconds and then on smooth for 45 seconds. In a blender, blend for 1–2 minutes or until smooth. Pour into glasses and serve.

Alternative Replace the sprouted broccoli seeds with either alfafa or fenugreek seeds.

Fruit Salad Detox Smoothie

As well as following a detox diet, for maximum benefit it is important to exercise on a regular basis. This helps to increase lymph gland activity and speed up the detox.

Ingredients

150 ml/¹/₄ pint orange juice

1 eating apple

1 ripe peach

small wedge of melon

few spinach leaves

small handful of flat leaf parsley

6 ice cubes

Method

Place the orange juice in a smoothie machine or blender. Core the apple and discard the peach stone. Discard the melon skin and seeds. Cut all the fruits into chunks and add to the orange juice with the spinach, parsley and ice cubes. If using a smoothie machine, blend on mix for 15 seconds and then on smooth for 45 seconds. In a blender, blend for 1–2 minutes or until smooth. Pour into glasses and serve.

Alternative Replace the spinach with rocket or sorrel leaves.

Tomato with Watermelon and Thyme

Choose plump, ripe and preferably organic tomatoes when making this drink, which is ideal for any time of the day. Thyme is good for counteracting excess sweating problems. Green tea helps in clearing up infections and improves the immune system, as well as helping the fight against heart disease and cancer.

Ingredients

4 tbsp freshly brewed green tea

225 g/8 oz ripe tomatoes

1 wedge watermelon (about $^1/_2$ a large watermelon)

small handful fresh thyme

few whole chive leaves

4 ice cubes

chive flowers, to decorate

Method

Cut the tomatoes into chunks and place in a smoothie machine or blender with the green tea. Discard the skin and seeds from the watermelon, cut into chunks and add to the tomatoes together with the thyme, chive leaves and ice cubes. If using a smoothie machine, blend on mix for 15 seconds and then on smooth for 45 seconds. In a blender, blend for 1–2 minutes or until smooth. Pour into glasses and, if liked, float a chive flower on top before serving.

Alternative Other melons can be used in place of the watermelon – try ogen or honeydew – and add an additional 150 ml/$^1/_4$ pint freshly brewed green tea as well.

Peaches and Oat Smoothie

Use ripe peaches for this drink – under-ripe fruits will not give you the best flavour, aroma or quantity. If ripe peaches are not available, use other stone fruits, such as nectarines, plums, damson or greengages.

Ingredients

4 ripe peaches

25 ml/1 fl oz aloe vera juice

150 ml/¼ pint probiotic bio-live natural yogurt

2 tbsp rolled oats

6 ice cubes

Method

Halve the peaches and discard the stones. Cut into chunks and place in a smoothie machine or blender with the aloe vera juice, yogurt, rolled oats and ice cubes. If using a smoothie machine, blend on mix for 15 seconds and then on smooth for 45 seconds. In a blender, blend for 1–2 minutes or until smooth. Pour into glasses and serve.

Alternative If liked, replace the aloe vera juice with cranberry juice, which is very beneficial for urinary infections. Aloe vera juice is slightly bitter, and if preferred add a little clear honey before blending.

Apple and Pear Smoothie

When choosing apples to make into smoothies, go for fruit that is sweet and juicy. This will ensure that the drink is sweet so there is no need to add any extra sugar. Probiotic bio–live yogurt is excellent for detoxifying, as well as keeping the digestive system healthy.

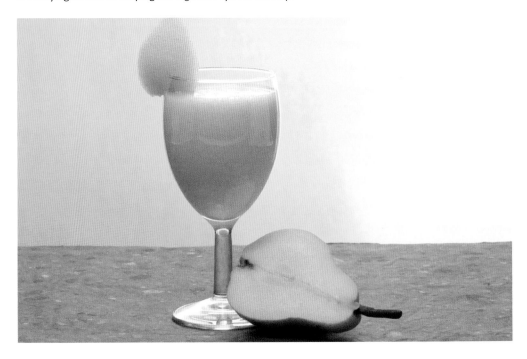

Ingredients

1 ripe apple, such as Gala

2 ripe pears, such as Conference

4 tbsp apple juice

2 tsp wheat grass powder

150 ml/¹/₄ pint probiotic bio–live natural yogurt

4 ice cubes

Method

Cut the apple and pears into quarters and discard the cores. Cut into chunks and place in a smoothie machine or blender with the apple juice, wheat grass powder, yogurt and ice cubes. If using a smoothie machine, blend on mix for 15 seconds and then on smooth for 45 seconds. In a blender, blend for 1–2 minutes or until smooth. Pour into glasses and serve immediately.

Alternative Use apple and cranberry juice together with the wheat grass powder for extra help fighting severe urinary infections.

Strawberry and Rosemary Smoothie

Just because you are following a detox diet, there is no need for the food or drink you consume to be unpleasant. The addition of fresh rosemary with the strawberries in this recipe enhances the memory as well as improving the circulatory system.

Ingredients

225 g/8 oz ripe strawberries

300 ml/¹/₂ pint organic bio–live strawberry yogurt

1–2 sprigs fresh rosemary

4 ice cubes

Method

Lightly rinse the strawberries and cut in half. Place in a smoothie machine or blender with the strawberry yogurt. Strip the leaves from the rosemary stalks and add the leaves with the ice cubes to the machine. If using a smoothie machine, blend on mix for 15 seconds and then on smooth for 45 seconds. In a blender, blend for 1–2 minutes or until smooth. Pour into glasses and serve.

Alternative Try other fruits and flavoured yogurts in place of the strawberries: raspberry, peach, or passion fruit with natural yogurt. If using passion fruit, sieve the flesh and seeds before using if a smoother texture is preferred.

Apricot with Kiwi Fruit and Peppermint

There are many varieties of mint, and peppermint is one of the most common – although spearmint could also be used here, if available. Peppermint is excellent for aiding digestion as well as for helping the liver and gall bladder.

Ingredients

225 g/8 oz fresh, ripe apricots

2 ripe gold or green kiwi fruits

85 ml/3 fl oz freshly brewed green tea

300 ml/¹/₂ pint organic apricot flavoured yogurt

few sprigs fresh peppermint

1 tbsp wheat germ

6 ice cubes

Method

Lightly rinse the apricots, cut in half and discard the stones. Place in a smoothie machine or blender together with the scooped out the flesh from the kiwi fruits and the green tea. Add the yogurt with the fresh peppermint sprigs, the wheat germ and ice cubes. If using a smoothie machine, blend on mix for 15 seconds and then on smooth for 45 seconds. In a blender, blend for 1–2 minutes or until smooth. Pour into glasses and serve.

Alternative Lightly poach ready-to-eat dried apricots in orange juice for 15–20 minutes until soft, then use as above. You can keep any remaining poached ready-to-eat dried apricots covered in the refrigerator for up to four days.

Orange, Lemon and Lime Juice

An incredibly quick and simple detox drink that can be enjoyed throughout the day is simply a slice of lemon or lime in a glass of freshly boiled water. This juice version will start the day off with a jolt and help to get rid of that sluggish feeling.

Ingredients

2 large oranges, preferably organic

juice of 1 lemon, preferably organic

juice of 1 lime, preferably organic

few fresh nettle leaves

150 ml/¹/₄ pint chilled, filtered water

Method

Peel the oranges, discarding the bitter white pith, and place in a smoothie machine or blender together with the lemon and lime juice. Lightly rinse the nettle leaves and add to the machine together with the cold, filtered water. If using a smoothie machine, blend on mix for 15 seconds and then on smooth for 45 seconds. In a blender, blend for 1–2 minutes or until smooth. Pour into glasses and serve.

Alternative Replace the nettle leaves with one tablespoon of wheat germ and add a few fresh sage leaves.

Peach and Passion Fruit Smoothie

When buying peaches or nectarines, choose fruits that feel ripe when lightly pressed and have a good aroma. Fruits which are bought under-ripe often do not ripen properly and go woody. If your peaches do not appear to be ripening well, poach lightly in a little honey and water. In this recipe, the yogurt will help the digestive system and the rolled oats will help if following a Glycemic Index diet.

Ingredients

2 large, ripe peaches

2 ripe passion fruits

85 ml/3 fl oz green tea

300 ml/¹/₂ pint probiotic bio-live natural yogurt

2 tbsp rolled oats

few fresh basil leaves

4 ice cubes

Method

Lightly rinse the peaches, cut in half and discard the stones. Place in a smoothie machine or blender. Scoop out the passion fruit pulp and seeds and sieve if a smoother texture is preferred. Place in the machine together with the green tea, yogurt, rolled oats, basil and ice cubes. If using a smoothie machine, blend on mix for 15 seconds and then on smooth for 45 seconds. In a blender, blend for 1–2 minutes or until smooth. Pour into glasses and serve.

Alternative If fresh peaches or nectarines are not available, try using damsons, making sure that all the fruits are sound and not forgetting to discard the stones.

Blueberries with Aloe Vera and Yogurt

Aloe vera is recognized as helping the body deal with constipation as well as many infections. The juice has a slightly bitter tang, so by combining it with yogurt in this recipe, the bitterness is not apparent.

Ingredients

150 g/5 oz fresh blueberries

25 ml/1 fl oz aloe vera juice

50 ml/2 fl oz elderflower cordial

300 ml/$^1/_2$ pint probiotic bio-live natural yogurt

1 tbsp flax oil

4 ice cubes

Method

Lightly rinse the blueberries and place in a smoothie machine or blender with the aloe vera juice, elderflower cordial, yogurt, flax oil and ice cubes. If using a smoothie machine, blend on mix for 15 seconds and then on smooth for 45 seconds. In a blender, blend for 1–2 minutes or until smooth. Pour into glasses and serve.

Alternative Add 100 g/4 oz raspberries to the blueberries and replace the natural yogurt with bio-live raspberry yogurt.

Tropical Cup with Echinacea

This is an ideal drink for gloomy winter days, that seem to last forever. The flavour of this drink will evoke long, hot, sunny days while the echinacea will help the body combat infections.

Ingredients

1 ripe mango

1 ripe papaya

1 large, ripe banana. peeled and cut into chunks

150 ml/¹/₄ pint unsweetened pineapple juice

few drops echinacea

6 ice cubes

Method

Peel the mango and papaya, discarding the stones and seeds and cutting the flesh into chunks. Place in a smoothie machine or blender together with the banana. Add the remaining ingredients, including the ice cubes. If using a smoothie machine, blend on mix for 15 seconds and then on smooth for 45 seconds. In a blender, blend for 1–2 minutes or until smooth. Pour the juice into glasses and serve.

Alternative Replace the pineapple juice and papaya with one ripe, medium pineapple that has been peeled, the hard central core discarded and the flesh cut into chunks. Add the same amount of apple juice.

Blackberry and Apple Smoothie

This smoothie uses flax seeds, which are rich in omega–3 fatty acids, and is ideal for vegetarians in particular. The addition of a few sprigs of lovage combined with the apples helps to eliminate excess fluid from the body.

Ingredients

2 ripe eating apples, such as Granny Smith
225 g/8 oz ripe blackberries
150 ml/¹/₄ pint unsweetened apple juice
150 ml/¹/₄ pint bio–live natural yogurt
1 tsp flax seeds
few sprigs of lovage

Method

Cut the apples into quarters and discard the cores, then cut the flesh into chunks. Lightly rinse the blackberries, hulling if necessary. Place the fruits into a smoothie machine or blender with the remaining ingredients. If using a smoothie machine, blend on mix for 15 seconds and then on smooth for 45 seconds. In a blender, blend for 1–2 minutes or until smooth. Pour into glasses and serve.

Alternative If lovage is unavailable, replace with parsley sprigs, tarragon or a few cleaned young nettle leaves – all will help eliminate excess fluid.

Courgette and Cucumber Smoothie

Serve this smoothie well chilled for maximum enjoyment: keeping the ingredients in the refrigerator and serving immediately will help. This smoothie is great for dealing with fluid retention.

Ingredients

1 whole hothouse cucumber

1 medium courgette

85 ml/3 fl oz green tea

300 ml/¹/₂ pint probiotic bio-live natural yogurt

few sprigs fresh parsley

2 sprigs fresh tarragon

3–4 whole chive leaves plus 2 chive flower heads, to decorate

4 ice cubes

Method

Peel the cucumber, discard the seeds and cut into chunks. Peel the courgette and cut into chunks. Place all the ingredients except the chive flower heads into a smoothie machine or blender. If using a smoothie machine, blend on mix for 15 seconds and then on smooth for 45 seconds. In a blender, blend for 1–2 minutes or until smooth. Pour into glasses, float the chive flower heads on top, if using, and serve.

Alternative Other herbs that can be used in this recipe that help to relieve fluid retention include parsley, lovage, nettles, dandelion and dock root.

Carrot with Apple and Sunflower Seeds

All edible seeds are a good source of energy and minerals. Both are required when following a detox diet.

Ingredients

225 g/8 oz carrots

1 large, ripe eating apple

300 ml/¹/₂ pint unsweetened apple juice

1 tbsp sunflower seeds

4 ice cubes

Method

Peel the carrots and cut into chunks. Discard the core from the apple and cut into chunks. Place in a smoothie machine or blender with the remaining ingredients, including the ice cubes. If using a smoothie machine, blend on mix for 15 seconds and then on smooth for 45 seconds. In a blender, blend for 1–2 minutes or until smooth. Pour into glasses and serve.

Alternative Use sesame or flax seeds in place of the sunflower seeds, or try a combination of all three.

Beetroot and Apple Smoothie

Try this smoothie to help stimulate the lymphatic system, You can use either raw or cooked beetroot in this recipe. Obviously using cooked beetroot is far easier than raw, but do ensure that you are using cooked beetroot that has not been steeped in vinegar, otherwise your smoothie will be very tart.

Ingredients

100 g/4 oz beetroot
2 ripe eating apples
85 ml/3 fl oz apple juice
small piece fresh root ginger
300 ml/1/2 pint probiotic bio–live natural yogurt
few shakes cayenne pepper

Method

Cut the beetroot into chunks, core the apples and cut into chunks. Peel the ginger and chop. Place in a smoothie machine together with the remaining ingredients. If using a smoothie machine, blend on mix for 15 seconds and then on smooth for 45 seconds. In a blender, blend for 1–2 minutes or until smooth. Pour into glasses and serve.

Alternative Replace the live yogurt with either cranberry or orange juice.

Broccoli with Orange and Mint

Broccoli is an excellent vegetable and provides a good source of fibre and antioxidants which help in the fight against cancer. Mint is a great detox ingredient, while orange is full of vitamin C. Combined, they offer an extremely healthy and delicious detox drink.

Ingredients

175 g/6 oz broccoli florets

85 ml/3 fl oz unsweetened orange juice

2 large oranges

2–3 sprigs fresh mint

1 tsp flax seeds

4 ice cubes

Method

Cut the broccoli into small florets and place in a smoothie machine or blender with the orange juice. Peel the oranges, discarding the bitter white pith, and divide into segments. Place in the machine with the remaining ingredients. If using a smoothie machine, blend on mix for 15 seconds and then on smooth for 45 seconds. In a blender, blend for 1–2 minutes or until smooth. Pour the juice into glasses and serve.

Alternative Omit the fresh oranges and increase the amount of unsweetened orange juice to 300 ml/$^1/_2$ pint. The smoothie will be thinner and more juice-like if not using fresh oranges.

Avocado with Watercress and Apple

The inclusion of avocado gives this drink a wonderfully smooth and lush feel, and is far healthier than you might think. Avocado is a good source of both vitamins and minerals, and combined with watercress and apple it has a dual effect, providing essential nutrients whilst also helping to detox the body.

Ingredients

1 large, ripe avocado

50 g/2 oz watercress sprigs

200 ml/7 fl oz unsweetened apple juice

2 tsp flax seeds

4 ice cubes

Method

Peel the avocado and discard the stone. Cut into chunks and place in a smoothie machine or blender and add the remaining ingredients. If using a smoothie machine, blend on mix for 15 seconds and then on smooth for 45 seconds. In a blender, blend for 1–2 minutes or until smooth. Pour into glasses and serve immediately

Alternative The watercress can be replaced with either rocket or sorrel leaves and a mixture of herbs, such as parsley, thyme, sage and chives. This will increase the detox effect of the drink.

Fennel with Orange and Wheat Germ

This drink has a very strong aniseed flavour which is provided by the fennel bulb. If fennel is unavailable, do not be tempted to replace it with extra herbs – use celery instead, which is similar to fennel but with a less pronounced flavour.

Ingredients
1 large or 2 small Florence fennel bulbs
150 ml/¹/₄ pint orange juice
1 large orange
1 tbsp wheat germ
few chive leaves plus 2 chive flower heads, to decorate
4 ice cubes

Method
Cut the fennel bulbs into small chunks, discarding the root. Place in a smoothie machine or blender with the orange juice. Peel the orange, discarding the bitter white pith, and divide into segments. Place in the machine with the wheat germ, chive leaves and ice cubes. If using a smoothie machine, blend on mix for 15 seconds and then on smooth for 45 seconds. In a blender, blend for 1–2 minutes or until smooth. Pour into glasses, float the chive heads on top, if using, and serve.

Alternative If preferred, use one small peeled and chopped onion in place of the chive leaves to aid detoxification.

Tomato, Apple and Basil Smoothie

This recipe is great when following a detox regime, and provided you use unsweetened apple juice, it will not matter if you use whole apples or juice – both work very well.

Ingredients

225 g/8 oz ripe tomatoes

1 eating apple

2 tsp finely grated orange rind

4 tbsp orange juice

few sprigs fresh basil

4 ice cubes

Method

Cut the tomatoes into chunks and place in a smoothie machine or blender with all the remaining ingredients. If using a smoothie machine, blend on mix for 15 seconds and then on smooth for 45 seconds. In a blender, blend for 1–2 minutes or until smooth. Pour into glasses and serve.

Alternative For a speedier drink, replace the fresh tomatoes with one 400 g can of chopped tomatoes, then add a few shakes of cayenne pepper before whizzing with the other ingredients.

Apple and Mint Smoothie

When using yogurt in a detox regime, ensure that you choose live yogurt as this will aid the digestion immensely. The fresh mint and apple in this recipe are great for the liver and gall bladder.

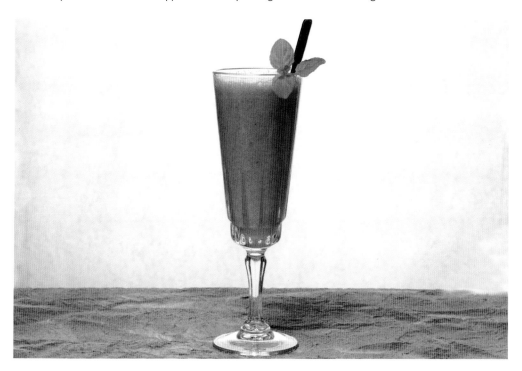

Ingredients

2 eating apples

85 ml/3 fl oz freshly brewed peppermint tea

$^1/_2$ large hothouse cucumber

300 ml/$^1/_2$ pint probiotic bio–live natural yogurt

1 tbsp wheat germ

few sprigs fresh mint plus 2 tiny sprigs to decorate

4 ice cubes

Method

Core the apples, cut into chunks and place in a smoothie machine or blender along with the tea. Peel the cucumber, discard the seeds and add to the apple together with the remaining ingredients. If using a smoothie machine, blend on mix for 15 seconds and then on smooth for 45 seconds. In a blender, blend for 1–2 minutes or until smooth. Pour into glasses, add the mint sprigs if using, and serve.

Alternative Use 1–2 tsp of wheat grass powder in place of the wheat germ.

Tomato and Sweet Pepper Smoothie

Try this smoothie with skinned peppers if time permits. Skinning peppers is easy – simply cut into quarters, discard the seeds and place skin–side uppermost under a preheated grill. Cook for 10 minutes or until the skins begin to blacken. Allow to cool, then peel them off.

Ingredients

225 g/8 oz ripe tomatoes
85 ml/3 fl oz freshly brewed green tea
1 large red pepper, skinned if preferred
1 small shallot
few sprigs of basil
6 ice cubes

Method

Cut the tomatoes into chunks and place in a smoothie machine together with the green tea. Discard the seeds from the peppers, cut into chunks and add to the tomatoes. Peel the shallot, chop and add to the machine together with the remaining ingredients. If using a smoothie machine, blend on mix for 15 seconds and then on smooth for 45 seconds. In a blender, blend for 1–2 minutes or until smooth. Pour into glasses and serve.

Alternative The shallot will give this smoothie a very distinct onion taste –
if preferred replace with chive leaves which like shallots and onion will also help combat fluid retention.

Watermelon and Ginger Smoothie

Watermelon is full of a delicious liquid whose flavour is intensified when combined with fresh ginger. It also provides a stimulant for the lymphatic system, as does the cayenne pepper used in this recipe.

Ingredients

1 large wedge watermelon (about $1/2$ a large
   watermelon)
small piece fresh root ginger
85 ml/3 fl oz ginger beer
few shakes cayenne pepper
4 ice cubes

Method

Cut away the skin from the watermelon and discard together with the seeds. Cut the flesh into chunks. Peel and roughly chop the ginger. Place all the ingredients into a smoothie machine or blender. If using a smoothie machine, blend on mix for 15 seconds and then on smooth for 45 seconds. In a blender, blend for 1–2 minutes or until smooth. Pour into glasses and serve,

Alternative If you are not keen on spicy tastes, omit the cayenne pepper and replace with a few sprigs of fresh oregano or the spiky leaves from two rosemary sprigs. Both are good for the lymphatic system.

Revitalising Refreshment

When feeling tired, most of us reach for an instant pick-me-up such as a chocolate bar or biscuit or a cup of coffee, and for a few minutes we are back to working at full tilt. But the energy burst does not last for long, and we would be do so much better for our bodies to take a couple of minutes and make a refreshing and revitalizing smoothie, crammed full of energy-giving foods.

We get our energy from the carbohydrates we consume of which there are two main sources: starch and sugar. Starchy foods are plant based: breakfast cereals, bread, potatoes, pulses and rice. Vegetables and a few fruits also contain starch in varying amounts. These starches are known as complex carbohydrates. Fruit also contains carbohydrate in the form of intrinsic sugar. The sugar found in chocolate bars, biscuits and sugar itself are known as free sugars, and help fractionally as a reviver but are also full of fats and calories and may encourage weight–gain. Ideally, we should consume 60 per cent of our daily carbohydrate requirements from complex carbs (in other words from vegetables and cereals) and 40 per cent from intrinsic sugar – fruit.

This section should make this goal simple. Choose from a delicious range of drinks, including Fig with Coconut and Banana Smoothie, Mango with Carrot and Lime or even Sweet Potato with Papaya. When feeling tired and jaded, forget the chocolate and make a smoothie.

Carrot and Watermelon Smoothie

When in need of a pick–me–up, look no further than this delicious drink crammed full of energizing calories that will help keep you going without piling on the pounds.

Ingredients

225 g/8 oz carrots

2 celery sticks

300 ml/¹/₂ pint orange juice

1 large wedge (about ¹/₂ large) watermelon

2–3 mint sprigs

4 ice cubes

2 celery sticks, for stirring

Method

Peel the carrots and chop. Trim the celery, chop and add both to a smoothie machine or blender together with the orange juice. Discard the skin and seeds from the watermelon, cut into chunks, and add to the carrots. If using a smoothie machine, blend on mix for 15 seconds and then on smooth for 45 seconds. In a blender, blend for 1–2 minutes or until smooth. Pour into glasses, place a celery stick in each and serve.

Alternative Other melons can be used if watermelon is not available. Use the flesh from at least half a melon – try honeydew or gallia. You will need a little more liquid, so choose either chilled mineral water or more ice cubes.

Beetroot with Parsnip and Chives

I would recommend using cooked beetroot for this drink, as it will make the drink quicker to make and far less messy. If using fresh beetroot, chop into small pieces and if using a smoothie machine, ensure that the liquid goes in at the beginning.

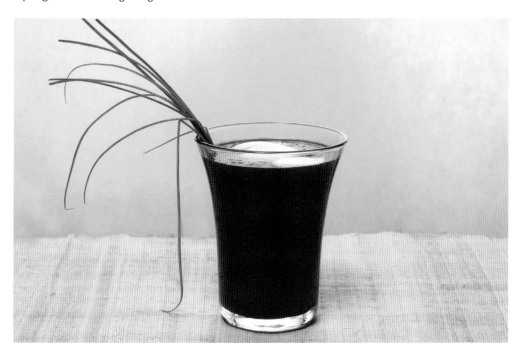

Ingredients

100 g/4 oz cooked beetroot

100 g/4 oz parsnip

300 ml/$\frac{1}{2}$ pint unsweetened apple juice

few fresh chive leaves

2 tbsp fromage frais or low fat live natural yogurt, to serve

1–2 tsp freshly snipped chives, to decorate

Method

Cut the beetroot into small chunks. Peel the parsnips, cut into small chunks and place both in a smoothie machine or blender with the apple juice and chives. If using a smoothie machine, blend on mix for 15 seconds and then on smooth for 45 seconds. In a blender, blend for 1–2 minutes or until smooth. Pour the juice into glasses, swirl with the fromage frais or yogurt, sprinkle with a few snipped chives and serve.

Alternative Replace the fromage frais with half fat crème fraîche and sprinkle the top with a little cayenne pepper

Broccoli with Orange and Parsnip

Purple sprouting broccoli is one of my favourite vegetables, most probably because it is seasonal and therefore a treat. Unlike the broccoli that is available all year round, purple sprouting broccoli has long spears and can be treated as asparagus. Use the whole spear, simply discarding any woody pieces. As with green broccoli it is full of antioxidants and fibre, offering a great source of energy–giving carbs.

Ingredients

175 g/6 oz purple sprouting broccoli
100 g/4 oz parsnips
300 ml/1$^1/_2$ pints unsweetened orange juice
1 tbsp fresh tarragon leaves
1 tbsp sesame seeds, to serve

Method

Trim the purple sprouting broccoli, discarding any woody pieces. Rinse thoroughly and chop. Peel the parsnip, chop into small chunks then place both in a smoothie machine with the orange juice and tarragon leaves. If using a smoothie machine, blend on mix for 15 seconds and then on smooth for 45 seconds. In a blender, blend for 1–2 minutes or until smooth. Pour into glasses, stir in the sesame seeds and serve.

Alternative   For a spicy drink add a little Tabasco or Worcestershire sauce.

Trio of Peppers

It is easy to find green, red, yellow and orange peppers as well as an excellent variety of chilli peppers. Here the peppers are teamed with tomatoes to give an instant energy boost.

Ingredients

1 yellow pepper
1 red pepper
1 orange pepper
1 chilli pepper, such as jalapeno or serrano
150 ml/¼ pint unsweetened apple juice
225 g/8 oz ripe tomatoes
4 ice cubes

Method

Cut all the peppers, except the chilli, into quarters, discard the seeds and roughly chop the flesh. Handling carefully, cut the chilli pepper in half and scoop out and discard the seeds and membrane. Place with the apple juice and peppers in a smoothie machine or blender. Chop the tomatoes and add to the peppers with the ice cubes. If using a smoothie machine, blend on mix for 15 seconds and then on smooth for 45 seconds. In a blender, blend for 1–2 minutes or until smooth. Pour into glasses and serve.

Alternative Chilli peppers are available in differing heat tolerances so choose one that suits your palate. The higher the heat tolerance number, the hotter the chilli, so if using chillies for the first time choose a chilli with a 3–5 rating.

Courgette with Red Pepper and Oats

The addition of oats in this drink will help to revitalize as they have a slow release of energy. You could also use fine or pin oatmeal if preferred, which would also work well.

Ingredients

225 g/8 oz courgettes
2 red peppers
150 ml/¼ pint unsweetened apple juice
4 ice cubes
2 tbsp rolled oats
2 celery sticks, to stir
few dashes sweet chilli sauce, to serve

Method

Trim the courgettes, cut into chunks and place in a smoothie machine or blender. Cut the peppers into quarters and discard the seeds. Cut into chunks and add to the courgettes together with the apple juice, ice cubes and oats. If using a smoothie machine, blend on mix for 15 seconds and then on smooth for 45 seconds. In a blender, blend for 1–2 minutes or until smooth. Pour into glasses. Place the celery sticks into the glasses and serve, with sweet chilli sauce served separately to those who want it.

Alternative In the summer months look for yellow courgettes, or use baby squashes such as acorn or custard.

Marrow with Avocado and Chilli

Avocados can only be bought fresh. Choose plump, undamaged fruits. Allow to ripen in the fruit bowl (not the refrigerator) and once cut, use immediately. Avocado contains vitamin E as well as other vitamins and minerals that play a good part in reviving the system.

Ingredients

$^1/_2$ small marrow (or use four 2.5 cm/1 in rings)

2 ripe avocados

50 ml/2 fl oz lime juice

150 ml/$^1/_4$ pint orange juice

1 chilli pepper

4 ice cubes

2 tbsp soured cream or live natural yogurt, to serve

Method

Peel the marrow, discard the seeds and cut into chunks. Cut the avocados in half, peel and discard the stones. Place the marrow, avocado, lime and orange juice in a smoothie machine or blender. Discard the seeds from the chilli pepper and add to the machine with the ice cubes. If using a smoothie machine, blend on mix for 15 seconds and then on smooth for 45 seconds. In a blender, blend for 1–2 minutes or until smooth. Pour into glasses, top with a spoonful of soured cream or yogurt and serve.

Alternative Replace the lime juice with all orange juice for a slightly sweeter drink. Courgettes can be used in place of the marrow.

127

Guacamole Smoothie

Guacamole is a traditional dip found in most parts of South America and offers a delicious accompaniment to many dishes. Try this smoothie in place of the dip either before or whilst eating dishes such as fajitas or chilli con carne.

Ingredients

2 ripe avocados

4 spring onions, trimmed and chopped

50 ml/2 fl oz lime or lemon juice

85 ml/3 fl oz orange juice

1 red pepper, deseeded

1–2 red chillies, depending on heat tolerance, deseeded

225 g/8 oz ripe tomatoes

$^1/_2$ hothouse cucumber, peeled

4 ice cubes

Method

Peel the avocados and discard the stones. Place in a smoothie machine or blender with the lime or lemon juice, orange juice and spring onions. Cut the pepper, chillies, tomatoes and cucumber into chunks and add to the machine with the ice cubes. If using a smoothie machine, blend on mix for 15 seconds and then on smooth for 45 seconds. In a blender, blend for 1–2 minutes or until smooth. Pour into glasses and serve.

Alternative Place a spoonful of soured cream or live natural yogurt on top and sprinkle the top with a few poppy seeds.

Creole Smoothie

Unfortunately this will have to be a seasonal drink, unless you live in an area where okra is readily available. Okra is full of soluble fibre which not only helps in controlling blood cholesterol levels, but will also give a big energy boost.

Ingredients

50 ml/2 fl oz lime juice

150 ml/¼ pint orange juice

175 g/6 oz carrots, peeled and chopped

75 g/3 oz okra, trimmed and chopped

225 g/8 oz ripe tomatoes, chopped

4 spring onions, trimmed and chopped

1 tbsp rolled oats

4 ice cubes

2 cleaned and trimmed celery sticks with leaves still attached, for stirring

Method

Place all the ingredients in a smoothie machine or blender, except the celery sticks. If using a smoothie machine, blend on mix for 15 seconds and then on smooth for 45 seconds. In a blender, blend for 1–2 minutes or until smooth. Pour into glasses, place a celery stick for stirring in each glass and serve immediately.

Alternative Add one deseeded and chopped chilli before blending or use a few dashes of Tabasco sauce to spice it up and kick-start your day.

Sweet Potato with Apple and Chives

Sweet potatoes are slightly overlooked by many people, which is a great shame. The sweet orange flesh combines well with many different flavours, and if following a Glycemic Index diet or just needing a quick pick-me-up, it is an excellent addition to the weekly shopping list.

Ingredients

225 g/8 oz sweet potato
2 celery sticks, trimmed
300 ml/$^1/_2$ pint unsweetened apple juice
small handful of fresh chives
2 ice cubes

Method

Peel the sweet potatoes and cut into chunks. Chop the celery then place both vegetables into a smoothie machine or blender. Add the apple juice and chives with the ice cubes. If using a smoothie machine, blend on mix for 15 seconds and then on smooth for 45 seconds. In a blender, blend for 1–2 minutes or until smooth. Pour into glasses and serve.

Alternative Yams could be used in place of the sweet potatoes and two ripe eating apples with mineral water in place of the apple juice.

Minty Pea and Cucumber Smoothie

You can choose how you drink this – either as a deliciously different drink, or a cold, refreshing soup in the summer. Whichever way you choose, it is guaranteed to be very popular.

Ingredients

225 g/8 oz sugar snaps

1 hothouse cucumber, peeled and cut into chunks

2 celery sticks, chopped

4 spring onions, trimmed and chopped

150 ml/^{1}/$_4$ pint semi–skimmed milk

handful fresh mint

4 ice cubes

chilled mineral water, to dilute

2–3 tbsp live natural yogurt, to serve

Method

Place all the ingredients except the mineral water and yogurt in a smoothie machine or blender. If using a smoothie machine, blend on mix for 15 seconds and then on smooth for 45 seconds. In a blender, blend for 1–2 minutes or until smooth. Pour into glasses, dilute if preferred, swirl with the yogurt and serve.

Alternative Use mangetout in place of the sugar snaps and replace the yogurt with a little single cream.

Watermelon with Okra and Coriander

The herb coriander is used extensively in many regions of the world to complement and enhance numerous diverse dishes. We in the West tend simply to use the leaves, discarding both the stalks and root of the herb. This is a great shame, as the entire herb is edible including the root, and once washed provides excellent flavour and aroma.

Ingredients

1 large wedge watermelon (about $^1/_2$ of a large fruit)

75 g/3 oz okra, trimmed

150 ml/$^1/_4$ pint tropical fruit juice

small handful coriander including stalks and root, well washed

50 g/2 oz ready-to-eat dried apricots

4 ice cubes

Method

Discard the skin and seeds from the watermelon and cut into chunks. Cut the okra in half and place with the melon flesh and fruit juice into a smoothie machine or blender. Add the coriander, the apricots and ice cubes. If using a smoothie machine, blend on mix for 15 seconds and then on smooth for 45 seconds. In a blender, blend for 1–2 minutes or until smooth. Pour into glasses and serve immediately.

Alternative Replace the apricots with dried figs, which have the same fibre content and are similarly good for the digestive system.

Fig, Coconut and Banana Smoothie

For maximum fibre content use either ready–to–eat fruits or dried figs. Soak them both in a little cooled boiled water for at least 15 minutes before using.

Ingredients

75 g/3 oz ready–to–eat dried figs, chopped

2 ripe bananas

300 ml/¹/₂ pint coconut milk

4 ice cubes

Method

Place the chopped figs into a smoothie machine or blender. Peel and cut the bananas into chunks and add to the machine with the coconut milk and ice cubes. If using a smoothie machine, blend on mix for 15 seconds and then on smooth for 45 seconds. In a blender, blend for 1–2 minutes or until smooth. Pour into glasses and serve.

Alternative Replace the bananas with the flesh from two ripe mangos and simply place all the ingredients into the machine and blend.

133

Sweet Potato with Papaya

When using papaya, ensure that the fruit is ripe for maximum flavour. Under-ripe fruit will lack both taste and aroma, as well as being quite dry and lacking in juice. Allow the fruit to ripen in a fruit bowl for 2–3 days before using.

Ingredients

100 g/4 oz sweet potato, peeled
2 ripe papayas
1 tsp finely grated lime rind
2 tbsp lime juice
300 ml/¹/₂ pint coconut milk
4 ice cubes

Method

Cut the sweet potatoes into chunks and place in a smoothie machine or blender. Peel the papayas and discard the seeds. Chop the flesh and add to the machine with the lime rind and juice, coconut milk and ice cubes. If using a smoothie machine, blend on mix for 15 seconds and then on smooth for 45 seconds. In a blender, blend for 1–2 minutes or until smooth. Pour into glasses and serve immediately.

Alternative Add a small handful of fresh coriander, including roots and stalks, to the machine before blending.

Melon with Blackcurrant and Ginger

Wheat grass is one of the latest herbs to hit our shelves and has many properties. Among other things it is an antioxidant and a great booster for the immune system. It comes from wheat grain that is allowed to sprout until it becomes young grass. It is then harvested and ground to form a powder.

Ingredients

$^1/_2$ small gallia melon

300 ml/$^1/_2$ pint blackcurrant juice or cordial

small piece root ginger

1–2 tsp clear honey, optional

2 pinches wheat grass powder

4 ice cubes

Method

Remove the skin and seeds from the melon and cut into chunks. Place in a smoothie machine or blender with the blackcurrant juice. Peel the ginger, chop and add to the machine with the honey if using, the wheat grass powder and the ice cubes. If using a smoothie machine, blend on mix for 15 seconds and then on smooth for 45 seconds. In a blender, blend for 1–2 minutes or until smooth. Pour into glasses and serve.

Alternative Replace the 300 ml/$^1/_2$ pint blackcurrant juice with the same amount of orange juice.

135

Pear and Blackcurrant Whizz

This drink is really quick and easy to make, ready in seconds and guaranteed to refresh instantly.

Ingredients

100 g/4 oz parsnip, peeled

2 ripe pears, such as Conference, cored

200 ml/7 fl oz blackcurrant juice or cordial

4 ice cubes

Method

Cut the parsnip and pears into chunks and place in a smoothie machine or blender with the blackcurrant juice and ice cubes. If using a smoothie machine, blend on mix for 15 seconds and then on smooth for 45 seconds. In a blender, blend for 1–2 minutes or until smooth. Pour into glasses and serve immediately.

Alternative Use plump, ripe blackcurrants in place of the juice and swirl with a little live natural yogurt.

Carrot with Apple and Alfalfa

It is very easy to sprout seeds such as alfalfa. If you do not have a sprouter, simply sprinkle some seeds onto a plate covered with a few sheets of kitchen paper and moisten with water, Leave for 3–5 days, keeping the seeds moist, before cutting and using. The ginger in this recipe is an excellent stimulant, especially root ginger.

Ingredients

175 g/6 oz carrots, peeled
1 ripe eating apple
300 ml/¹/₂ pint ginger ale
1 small piece root ginger
2 tbsp sprouted alfalfa seeds
crushed ice

Method

Cut the carrots into chunks, core the apples, cut into chunks and place both in a smoothie machine or blender with the ginger ale. Peel the ginger and cut into small chunks; add to the machine together with the alfalfa seeds and two tablespoons of crushed ice. If using a smoothie machine, blend on mix for 15 seconds and then on smooth for 45 seconds. In a blender, blend for 1–2 minutes or until smooth. Pour into glasses and serve.

Alternative If alfalfa seeds are not available, use other seeds such as fenugreek or bean sprouts.

Red Cabbage with Celery and Carrot

Red cabbage is more readily available in the winter months than the summer. When using, it is advisable to wash thoroughly in plenty of cold water and continue until the water runs clear. Discard any damaged or outside leaves.

Ingredients

100 g/4 oz raw red cabbage
3 celery sticks, trimmed
100 g/4 oz carrots, peeled
2 tbsp rolled oats
300 ml/$^1/_2$ pint orange juice
4 ice cubes

Method

Cut the cabbage into chunks, discarding the tough central stalk and the outer leaves. Cut the celery and carrots into chunks and place all the vegetables into a smoothie machine or blender. Add the oats with the orange juice and ice cubes. If using a smoothie machine, blend on mix for 15 seconds and then on smooth for 45 seconds. In a blender, blend for 1–2 minutes or until smooth. Pour into glasses and serve.

Alternative Replace the red cabbage with white cabbage and use unsweetened apple juice rather than orange.

Dates with Sweet Potato and Tomatoes

Use fresh dates if available: although their carbohydrate content is not as high as dried, they are complimented by the addition of the sweet potatoes.

Ingredients

50 g/2 oz fresh or dried dates
175 g/6 oz sweet potato, peeled
100 g/4 oz ripe tomatoes
300 ml/¹/₂ pint orange juice
small handful fresh coriander
4 ice cubes

Method

Cut the dates in half and discard the stones. Cut the sweet potato and tomatoes into chunks and place in a smoothie machine or blender with the dates. Add the orange juice with the coriander and ice cubes. If using a smoothie machine, blend on mix for 15 seconds and then on smooth for 45 seconds. In a blender, blend for 1–2 minutes or until smooth. Pour into glasses and serve.

Alternative The dates can be replaced with dried or fresh apricots, or use a combination of both.

Broccoli with Sweet Potato and Chives

When you need to recharge the batteries, look no further than this unusual but delicious drink. It will hit the spot instantly and leave you feeling like new.

Ingredients

100 g/4 oz broccoli florets
100 g/4 oz sweet potatoes, peeled
2 celery sticks, chopped
300 ml/¹/₂ pint apple and cranberry juice
small handful chive leaves
4 ice cubes

Method

Thoroughly wash the broccoli florets, chop the sweet potatoes into chunks and place both in a smoothie machine or blender along with the remaining ingredients. If using a smoothie machine, blend on mix for 15 seconds and then on smooth for 45 seconds. In a blender, blend for 1–2 minutes or until smooth. Pour into glasses and serve.

Alternative Replace the broccoli florets with cauliflower florets and add a few dried cranberries.

Melon and Elderflower Reviver

Elderflower has a very delicate flavour and combines well with other fruits such as melon, apple, lemon or lime.

Ingredients

¹/₂ ripe gallia melon

85 ml/3 fl oz elderflower cordial

4 ice cubes

iced sparkling water, to serve

2 lemon slices, to decorate

Method

Discard the skin and seeds from the melon, cut into chunks and place in a smoothie machine or blender. Add the elderflower cordial and ice cubes. If using a smoothie machine, blend on mix for 15 seconds and then on smooth for 45 seconds. In a blender, blend for 1–2 minutes or until smooth. Pour into glasses and top up with the iced sparkling water. Decorate the glasses with a lemon slice and serve.

Alternative   Try using two peeled oranges or two cored eating apples in place of the melon.

Mango with Carrot and Lime

Mango is extremely rich in fibre, particularly soluble fibre, as well as being an excellent source of vitamin E. It is therefore an ideal choice for revitalizing.

Ingredients

2 ripe mangos

100 g/4 oz carrots

1–2 tsp finely grated lime rind

85 ml/3 fl oz lime juice

150 ml/^{1}/$_4$ pint orange juice

4 ice cubes

chilled mineral water, to dilute

Method

Peel the mangos and slice the flesh away from the stone. Peel the carrots and cut into chunks. Place the mango flesh and carrots with the lime rind and juices in a smoothie machine or blender with the ice cubes. If using a smoothie machine, blend on mix for 15 seconds and then on smooth for 45 seconds. In a blender, blend for 1–2 minutes or until smooth. Pour into glasses, dilute to taste and serve.

Alternative Replace the carrots with one eating apple, and add 85 ml/3 fl oz apple juice and ^{1}/$_2$ tsp ground cinnamon in place of the lime rind and juice. Place a long cinnamon stick in each glass to use as a stirrer.

Pineapple Crush

Surprisingly, pineapple does not contain much fibre. However, there is plenty of fibre in this recipe due to the inclusion of banana and papaya. Pineapple does contain plenty of bromelain, an enzyme that helps to break down protein which aids digestion. This is a great drink if you are feeling sluggish.

Ingredients

1 medium, ripe pineapple
300 ml/^{1}/$_2$ pint freshly brewed ginseng tea
1 ripe banana
1 ripe papaya
1 tbsp rolled oats
4 ice cubes

Method

Discard the plume and skin from the pineapple, cut into quarters and discard the hard central core. Cut into chunks and place in a smoothie machine or blender together with the tea. Peel the banana and papaya and discard the seeds. Cut the flesh into chunks, add to the machine and add the oats, sprouted seeds and ice cubes. If using a smoothie machine, blend on mix for 15 seconds and then on smooth for 45 seconds. In a blender, blend for 1–2 minutes or until smooth. Pour into glasses and serve.

Alternative Add some highly nutritional sprouted seeds to the smoothie – try either fenugreek, alfalfa or mung beans.

143

Grapefruit Refresher

It is now possible to buy three different colours of grapefruit: red, pink and the traditional yellow variety. The red and pink are sweeter than the yellow, and by using all three, you will create a refreshing and stimulating drink which should not need any extra sweetness.

Ingredients

1 red grapefruit
1 pink grapefruit
1 yellow grapefruit
300 ml/¹/₂ pint orange juice
1–2 pinches blue–grass algae powder
4 ice cubes
sparkling water, to dilute

Method

Peel all the grapefruits and divide into segments. Place in a smoothie machine or blender with the orange juice, blue–grass algae and ice cubes. If using a smoothie machine, blend on mix for 15 seconds and then on smooth for 45 seconds. In a blender, blend for 1–2 minutes or until smooth. Pour into glasses and serve diluted with water to taste.

Alternative Oranges can be used in place of the yellow grapefruit to provide a slightly sweeter drink. Replace the orange juice with grapefruit to give it a little more kick. A little clear honey could be added as well if liked.

Breakfast Delight

Give your system a kick start with this delicious drink – guaranteed to get you going and keep you going until lunchtime.

Ingredients

2 pink grapefruit
1 large orange
1 ripe papaya
300 ml/$^1/_2$ pint red grapefruit juice
1–2 tbsp muesli
pinch of kelp powder
4 ice cubes
sparkling mineral water, to serve

Method

Peel the grapefruit and orange and divide into segments. Peel the papaya, discard the seeds and cut into chunks. Place all the fruits with the juice, muesli, kelp powder and ice cubes in a smoothie machine or blender. If using a smoothie machine, blend on mix for 15 seconds and then on smooth for 45 seconds. In a blender, blend for 1–2 minutes or until smooth. Pour into glasses, top up with sparkling water and serve.

Alternative Replace the muesli with a sugar–free homemade version – rolled oats, a few dried fruits such as raisins or sultanas and a few toasted flaked almonds.

Fig and Orange Smoothie

If using dried figs, look for the ready-to-eat dried figs, as they will blend more quickly than fresh figs. Here the figs are combined with orange and passion fruit, creating an aromatic and refreshing drink.

Ingredients

4–6 ripe fresh figs, depending on size, or 75 g/3 oz
    ready-to-eat dried figs, chopped

150 ml/¹/₄ pint mixed orange and apple juice

2 large oranges

1 ripe passion fruit

1–2 pinches of spirulina powder

4 ice cubes

chilled mineral water, to dilute

Method

Place the figs in a smoothie machine or blender together with the fruit juice. Peel the oranges, divide into segments and add to the machine. Scoop the flesh and seeds from the passion fruit, sieve the flesh if a smoother texture is preferred, then add to the machine with the spirulina powder and ice cubes. If using a smoothie machine, blend on mix for 15 seconds and then on smooth for 45 seconds. In a blender, blend for 1–2 minutes or until smooth. Pour into glasses, dilute to taste with the mineral water and serve.

Alternative The figs can be replace with ready-to-eat dried or fresh apricots.
If using fresh, cut in half and discard the stones then proceed as above.

Beetroot, Pear and Apple Reviver

This great recipe is packed full of energy-giving produce that will help to revive you and keep you going throughout the day.

Ingredients

100 g/4 oz cooked beetroot
1 eating apple, such as Granny Smith
1 large, ripe pear, such as Conference
2–3 tsp clear honey
300 ml/¹/₂ pint apple juice

Method

Cut the beetroot into chunks and place in a smoothie machine or blender. Peel the apple and pear, discard the cores and cut into chunks. Add to the machine together with the honey and apple juice. If using a smoothie machine, blend on mix for 15 seconds and then on smooth for 45 seconds. In a blender, blend for 1–2 minutes or until smooth. Pour into glasses and serve.

Alternative Replace the apples with oranges and use orange juice instead of the apple juice.

Red and Green Whizz

Here, red and green grapes are used with plump, lush cherries, which are bursting with flavour. Cherries have a limited season, so take advantage of them when around and enjoy this fabulous pick-me-up.

Ingredients

100 g/4 oz seedless red grapes

100 g/4 oz seedless green grapes

100 g/4 oz ripe cherries

150 ml/¼ pint freshly brewed ginseng tea

4 ice cubes, to serve

Method

Rinse the grapes and remove any stalks, then place in a smoothie machine or blender. Stone the cherries and add to the grapes together with the ginseng tea. If using a smoothie machine, blend on mix for 15 seconds and then on smooth for 45 seconds. In a blender, blend for 1–2 minutes or until smooth. Place the ice cubes into two glasses, add the smoothie and serve.

Alternative For a more indulgent drink, top each filled glass with a spoonful of live cherry flavoured yogurt and sprinkle with a little grated chocolate.

Orange with Wheat Grass and Yogurt

Wheat grass can be used in the diet for a variety of reasons. It acts as a natural tonic to the system as well as being a good for detoxification. Here it is combined with oranges and is perfect for an early morning start.

Ingredients

1 large orange

juice of 1 lemon

150 ml/$^1/_4$pint orange or mandarin juice

1 tsp clear honey, optional

1 pinch wheat grass powder

150 ml/$^1/_4$ pint bio–live natural yogurt

4 ice cubes

Method

Peel the orange and divide into segments. Place in a smoothie machine or blender. Squeeze the juice from the lemon and add to the machine together with the orange or mandarin juice, clear honey if using and the wheat grass powder. If using a smoothie machine, blend on mix for 15 seconds and then on smooth for 45 seconds. In a blender, blend for 1–2 minutes. Add the yogurt and ice cubes and whizz for a further 20–40 seconds in a smoothie machine or a further minute in a blender, or until smooth. Pour into glasses and serve.

Alternative Replace the orange with one pink grapefruit and if a slightly sweeter drink is preferred, add a little extra honey. Do taste first before adding more honey.

Honeydew Melon with Brussels Sprouts

Brussels sprouts can now be bought all year round, but in the summer they will be frozen. They are crammed full of fibre as well vitamin C, and provide the right amount of nutrients to refresh in this unusual drink. Try it – you might be surprised!

Ingredients

$^1/_2$ small honeydew melon

100 g/4 oz Brussels sprouts, trimmed

200 ml/7 fl oz cooled green tea

2 tbsp muesli

4 ice cubes

Method

Peel the melon, discard the seeds and cut the flesh into chunks. Place in a smoothie machine or blender. Slice the Brussels sprouts in half then add to the machine with the tea, muesli and ice cubes. If using a smoothie machine, blend on mix for 15 seconds and then on smooth for 45 seconds. In a blender, blend for 1–2 minutes or until smooth. Pour into glasses and serve.

Alternative Spoon a little live natural yogurt on top and sprinkle with a few freshly snipped chives.

Pomegranate and Grape Smoothie

Take advantage of pomegranates when they are around, as their season in Europe is very short. They can be found in abundance in the Middle East and tropical countries.

Ingredients

2 ripe pomegranates

175 g/ 6 oz seedless green grapes

6 fresh or dried dates, stoned

300 ml/¹/₂ pint orange juice

1–2 pinches of spirulina powder

2–3 crushed cardamom pods

4 ice cubes

Method

Cut the pomegranates in half and scoop out the seeds into a blender. Add the grapes with the dates, the orange juice, spirulana powder, crushed cardamom pods and ice cubes. Whizz in a blender for 1–2 minutes or until smooth. If a smooth texture is preferred, pass through a nylon sieve to remove the pomegranate seeds. Pour into glasses and serve.

Alternative If fresh pomegranates are not available, replace both the fruit and orange juice with grenadine juice – grenadine is made from fresh pomegranates.

151

Pomelo and Mandarin Smoothie

Pomelos are the largest of the citrus fruits and have a thick, pale green skin. The flesh is similar to grapefruit, slightly more tart and often in need of a little extra sweetness. Combined with mandarins – small fruits with an easy to peel skin and sweet flesh – the flavours balance each other out.

Ingredients
1 pomelo

3 mandarins

150 ml/¹/₄ pint freshly brewed green tea

2 tbsp muesli

1 pinch blue–grass algae powder

4 ice cubes

Method
Peel the pomelo, discarding the bitter white pith, and divide into segments. Peel the mandarins, discard pips if necessary and place both fruits in a smoothie machine or blender along with the green tea, muesli, blue–grass algae and ice cubes. If using a smoothie machine, blend on mix for 15 seconds and then on smooth for 45 seconds. In a blender, blend for 1–2 minutes or until smooth. Pour into glasses and serve.

Alternative Use other fruits in place of the pomelo if liked; try a mixture of pink, red or yellow grapefruit or one medium, ripe pineapple.

Kiwi Fruits with Blueberries

Use either green or gold kiwis or a mixture of both in this drink. Kiwi fruits contain high levels of vitamin C and provide a refreshing, instant pick-me-up when blended into a drink.

Ingredients

2 green kiwi fruits

2 gold kiwi fruits

150 ml/¹/₄ pint bio-live natural yogurt

100 g/4 oz blueberries

1 tbsp flax oil

4 ice cubes

Method

Scoop the flesh from each kiwi fruit and place in a smoothie machine or blender along with the remaining ingredients, including the ice cubes. If using a smoothie machine, blend on mix for 15 seconds and then on smooth for 45 seconds. In a blender, blend for 1–2 minutes or until smooth. Pour into glasses and serve.

Alternative The blueberries can be replaced with raspberries or strawberries, if liked.

Summer Specials

Everyone loves summer, and whether you're in the middle of long winter months looking forward to the thought of hot, sunny days, or you're in the midst of summer and want to relax with long, cooling drinks, this is the section for you.

This chapter shows how to make deliciously creamy smoothies, packed full of summer fruits, sodas full of luscious, cooling ice cream, and shakes that take advantage of both milk and yogurt. Whatever your age you will find something for everyone. Try a Peanut Butter Smoothie, packed full of banana, peanut butter and chocolate ice cream, or a Frosty Fruit Smoothie with passion fruit, melon and grapes. For a refreshing change try a semi-frozen drink such as Watermelon Semi-Freddo, or a delicious Blackcurrant Granita. There really is something for everyone here, so make a smoothie or two and enjoy the summer all year round.

Summer Special Soda

Summer is a time full of lush fruits and vegetables, bursting with sun, vitamins and flavour. Make sure that the fruits you use are perfectly ripe for maximum taste and flavour.

Ingredients

85 ml/3 fl oz orange juice

$^1/_2$ small, ripe gallia melon

175 g/6 oz fresh raspberries

1 tsp finely grated orange rind

2 scoops good quality vanilla ice cream, to serve

soda water, to serve

Method

Place the orange juice in a smoothie machine or blender. Peel the melon, discard the seeds and cut the flesh into chunks. Add to the smoothie machine or blender with the raspberries and orange rind. If using a smoothie machine, blend on mix for 15 seconds and then on smooth for 45 seconds. In a blender, blend for 1–2 minutes or until smooth. Pour into glasses and place a scoop of ice cream in each glass. Top up with soda water and serve immediately.

Alternative Try using raspberry ripple or chocolate ice cream in place of the vanilla, or a combination of both.

Tangy Summer Sensation

Bursting with colour and full of tangy flavours, this smoothie is bound to be a big hit at any time of the year.

Ingredients

$^1/_2$ cantaloupe melon

1 ripe papaya

175 g/6 oz carrots

4 tbsp orange juice

4 ice cubes

Method

Peel the melon and papaya, discard the seeds cut into chunks. Cut the carrots into chunks. Place all the ingredients in a smoothie machine or blender with the ice cubes. If using a smoothie machine, blend on mix for 15 seconds and then on smooth for 45 seconds. In a blender, blend for 1–2 minutes or until smooth. Pour into glasses and serve.

Alternative Add four fresh, ripe, stoned apricots if available in place of the papaya.

Banana and Raspberry Smoothie

This nourishing smoothie will help sustain you throughout the day. Not only is it full of energy–rich fruits, it also contains tofu which will keep you feeling energized.

Ingredients

2 ripe bananas
225 g/8 oz fresh raspberries
75 g/3 oz tofu, drained
150 ml/¹/₄ pint orange juice
4 ice cubes

Method

Peel the bananas, cut into chunks and place in a smoothie machine or blender with the remaining ingredients. If using a smoothie machine, blend on mix for 15 seconds and then on smooth for 45 seconds. In a blender, blend for 1–2 minutes or until smooth. Pour into glasses and serve.

Alternative Other fruits can be used in place of the raspberries – try blueberries, tayberries, loganberries

Peanut Butter Bliss

It is your choice whether you use crunchy peanut butter or smooth in this recipe. Although relatively high in calories, an occasional treat is a good idea as it helps to lift the spirits and give a general feeling of well-being. Nuts also contain important nutrients.

Ingredients

4 tbsp orange juice

3 tbsp crunchy or smooth peanut butter

1 ripe banana, chopped

2 tbsp lemon juice

2 scoops chocolate ice cream

2 scoops vanilla ice cream, to serve

rolled chocolate–filled wafer biscuits, to serve

Method

Place the orange juice, peanut butter, banana, lemon juice and chocolate ice cream in a smoothie machine or blender. If using a smoothie machine, blend on mix for 15 seconds and then on smooth for 45 seconds. In a blender, blend for 1–2 minutes or until smooth. Pour into glasses and add a scoop of vanilla ice cream to each glass and put a wafer biscuit in each scoop. Serve immediately.

Alternative Replace the ice cream with scoops of frozen strawberry yogurt or raspberry sorbet. and add a few fresh strawberries or raspberries to the machine prior to blending.

Frosty Fruit Smoothie

During the summer months when a cold frosty smoothie is called for, it is a good idea to keep a variety of fruits in the refrigerator, so that a refreshing drink can be whizzed up in seconds.

Ingredients

175 g/6 oz chilled, seedless green grapes
2 ripe passion fruits
$^1/_2$ small ogen or cantaloupe melon, chilled
150 ml/$^1/_4$ pint chilled apple juice
4 ice cubes

Method

Rinse the grapes and discard any stalks and place in a smoothie machine or blender. Scoop the flesh and seeds from the passion fruits, sieve if a smooth texture is preferred, and add to the machine. Discard the skin and seeds from the melon and cut into chunks. Place all the remaining ingredients in the machine. If using a smoothie machine, blend on mix for 15 seconds and then on smooth for 45 seconds. In a blender, blend for 1–2 minutes or until smooth. Pour into cold glasses and serve.

Alternative Other chilled juices can be used in place of the apple juice. Apple and cranberry or apple and mango juice work particularly well.

Tropical Fruit Smoothie

Pineapple contains bromelain which helps to balance the acidity and alkalinity levels in the digestive system. Although coconut milk contains saturated fat, research indicates that it is not nearly as harmful as fat from animal and dairy products.

Ingredients

1 large, ripe avocado
2 tbsp lime juice
1 medium, ripe pineapple
1 tsp clear honey
150 ml/^{1}/$_4$ pint chilled coconut milk
4 ice cubes
2 scoops chocolate ice cream, to serve

Method

Peel the avocado, discard the stone, cut the flesh into chunks and sprinkle with the lime juice. Cut the plume and skin off the pineapple and discard. Cut into quarters and discard the hard central core. Cut the flesh into chunks. Place all the ingredients except the ice cream in a smoothie machine or blender. If using a smoothie machine, blend on mix for 15 seconds and then on smooth for 45 seconds. In a blender, blend for 1–2 minutes or until smooth. Pour into glasses, top with the ice cream and serve immediately.

Alternative Omit the pineapple and use any other tropical fruits instead. Papayas, passion fruits or mangos would all work well in this recipe.

161

Chilled Apple and Blackberry Smoothie

Apples are universally popular and have great health benefits. They are full of vitamin C with a low glycemic index, which helps to keep hunger pangs at bay.

Ingredients

2 fresh eating apples

4 tbsp apple juice

150 g/5 oz chilled fresh or frozen blackberries

300 ml/$^1/_2$ pint live natural yogurt

4 mint sprigs

2 scoops toffee pecan or vanilla ice cream, to serve

2 mint sprigs, to decorate

4 fresh blackberries or 2 apple wedges, to decorate

Method

Rinse the apples, core and cut into chunks. Place the apple juice, chopped apples, blackberries, yogurt and mint in a smoothie machine or blender. If using a smoothie machine, blend on mix for 15 seconds and then on smooth for 45 seconds. In a blender, blend for 1–2 minutes or until smooth. Pour into glasses, top with the ice cream and decorate the top with the remaining mint sprigs and ripe blackberries.

Alternative Raspberries or strawberries can replace the blackberries.
If using strawberries, use chilled rather than frozen, but the raspberries can be chilled or frozen.

Chilly Cherry

Growing cherries can be very labour intensive, which is most probably why they are one of the most expensive fruits available. They are seldom seen frozen, normally only found in packs of mixed frozen fruits – don't be put off using these packs. They provide all the nutrients you would get from ripe fruits and are a great standby for long, hot summer days.

Ingredients

500 g pack frozen mixed fruits containing cherries, blackberries, raspberries and strawberries, beginning to thaw

300 ml/^{1}/$_2$ pint apple and cranberry juice

2 spoonfuls frozen raspberry or lemon sorbet

Method

Place all the ingredients in a smoothie machine or blender. If using a smoothie machine, blend on mix for 15 seconds and then on smooth for 45 seconds. In a blender, blend for 1–2 minutes or until smooth and 'slushy'. Pour into glasses and serve immediately.

Alternative Use packs of single fruits, such as raspberries or even cranberries. Cranberries may need a little clear honey to sweeten, as they are very tart when ripe.

Strawberry Slush

Strawberries are now readily available all year round, coming from many countries worldwide. When locally grown strawberries are available, use these however, as the flavour will be far superior to those that have been picked slightly under–ripe. Locally grown berries are allowed to ripen on the plant, thus enjoying more of the sun, and have much more flavour.

Ingredients

450 g/1 lb fresh strawberries, hulled

1 tbsp balsamic vinegar

3 tbsp orange juice

4 ice cubes

Method

Lightly rinse the strawberries and leave to drain. Place on a tray and sprinkle with the balsamic vinegar and leave for at least 5 minutes. Place the strawberries and any juice together with the orange juice and ice cubes in a smoothie machine or blender. If using a smoothie machine, blend on mix for 15 seconds and then on smooth for 45 seconds. In a blender, blend for 1–2 minutes or until smooth and a 'slush' is formed. Pour into glasses and serve immediately.

Alternative Look for white balsamic vinegar in place on the traditional balsamic vinegar.
Or use a few twists of freshly ground black pepper instead.

Summer Cooler

When it is hot and sunny, there are times when all you want is a long, cool drink to help you unwind and relax. Try this – guaranteed to cool you down in seconds.

Ingredients

1 large wedge of watermelon
100 g/4 oz ripe strawberries
1 ripe banana
3 tbsp elderflower cordial
few sprigs fresh coriander
4 ice cubes

Method

Discard the skin and seeds from the watermelon and cut into chunks. Lightly rinse the strawberries and peel the banana, cutting it into large chunks. Place the fruits and elderflower cordial with the ice cubes in a smoothie machine or blender. If using a smoothie machine, blend on mix for 15 seconds and then on smooth for 45 seconds. In a blender, blend for 1–2 minutes or until smooth and a 'slush' is formed. Pour into glasses and serve immediately. If liked, add a few extra ice cubes to each glass

Alternative In place of the ice cubes, add two large scoops of strawberry ice cream before blending.

165

Pear and Maple Swirl

This delicious smoothie can be mixed and matched according to personal tastes. We all need a little indulgence occasionally, and the maple syrup in this recipe adds that finishing touch.

Ingredients

2 large, ripe dessert pears such as Williams
  or Conference
1 tsp finely grated orange rind
300 ml/^{1}/$_2$ pint live natural yogurt
2 scoops toffee–flavoured or vanilla ice cream, to serve
1–2 tbsp maple syrup, to serve

Method

Peel and core the pears, chop and place in a smoothie machine or blender with the orange rind and yogurt. If using a smoothie machine, blend on mix for 15 seconds and then on smooth for 45 seconds. In a blender, blend for 1–2 minutes or until smooth. Pour into glasses and top with the ice cream. Swirl with a little maple syrup and serve immediately.

Alternative Use chocolate ice cream and swirl with a little melted white chocolate.

Eastern Delight

Canned lychees are blended with Eastern spices in this recipe to make an aromatic smoothie with a hint of the Orient.

Ingredients

300 ml/$^1/_2$ pint coconut milk

400 g can lychees, drained

2 cardamom pods

1 lemon grass stalk

1 small piece star anise

2 scoops vanilla ice cream, to serve

Method

Place the coconut milk with the drained fruits in a smoothie machine or blender. Place the cardamom pods in a pestle and pound with a mortar to remove the seeds. Place the seeds in the machine. Remove the outer leaves from the lemon grass, chop, then pound with the star anise until as fine as possible. Add to the machine. If using a smoothie machine, blend on mix for 15 seconds and then on smooth for 45 seconds. In a blender, blend for 1–2 minutes or until smooth. Pour into glasses, top with the ice cream and serve immediately.

Alternative You will find that the small pieces of spice will sink to the bottom of the drink, but you can sieve the liquid if wanted. Use live natural yogurt in place of the coconut milk if preferred.

Black Forest Smoothie

This smoothie is based on the very famous chocolate cake from Germany that has a rich chocolate sponge, lashes of cream and lush, ripe cherries. This version is definitely healthier!

Ingredients

175 g/6 oz fresh, ripe cherries

300 ml/¹/₂ pint black cherry yogurt

150 ml/¹/₄ pint semi–skimmed milk

4 ice cubes

2 scoops chocolate ice cream, to serve

1 tbsp finely grated milk or white chocolate, to decorate

Method

Rinse the cherries, reserve 2–4 and stone the rest. Place the fruit in a smoothie machine or blender with the yogurt, milk and ice cubes. If using a smoothie machine, blend on mix for 15 seconds and then on smooth for 45 seconds. In a blender, blend for 1–2 minutes or until smooth. Pour into glasses, add a scoop of ice cream to both and sprinkle with a little chocolate. Top with the reserved cherries and serve.

Alternative Whizz the smoothie with the ice cream and omit the ice cubes, then top with a swirl of lightly whipped cream.

Rhubarb Fool

Any fruits can be used to make this delicious smoothie, although rhubarb is the traditional fruit used in fools and crumbles. Rhubarb is rich in calcium but the acidic content in the fruit can hinder its absorption. Add a little ginger, honey or sugar to counteract the tartness and help with the absorption.

Ingredients

350 g/12 oz rhubarb

85 ml/3 fl oz ginger wine

1–2 tbsp clear honey, or to taste

300 ml/$^1/_2$ pint freshly made custard

$^1/_2$ tsp powdered ginger

2 scoops vanilla ice cream, to serve

Method

Trim the rhubarb and cut into chunks. Place all the ingredients except the ice cream in a smoothie machine or blender. If using a smoothie machine, blend on mix for 15 seconds and then on smooth for 45 seconds. In a blender, blend for 1–2 minutes or until smooth. Pour into glasses, top each with a scoop of ice cream and serve.

Alternative Use a drained 400 g can of rhubarb and omit the ginger wine.
Add honey to taste if liked and top with a little chopped stem ginger.

Fragrant Peach Smoothie

Both peaches and nectarines are available as white and yellow fleshed varieties, the yellow varieties being the most common. Whichever you use, do ensure that the fruit is at it best – ripe and juicy.

Ingredients

2 ripe peaches
2 ripe passion fruits
300 ml/$^1/_2$ pint peach and passion fruit yogurt
few drops vanilla extract
2 scoops passion fruit or raspberry sorbet, to serve

Method

Cut the peaches in half, discard the stones and place in a smoothie machine or blender. Reserve half a passion fruit. Scoop out the flesh and seeds from the remaining passion fruits and sieve if a smoother texture is preferred. Add to the machine with the yogurt and vanilla extract. If using a smoothie machine, blend on mix for 15 seconds and then on smooth for 45 seconds. In a blender, blend for 1–2 minutes or until smooth. Pour into glasses and top with the sorbet. Spoon a little of the reserved passion fruit flesh and seeds on top and serve.

Alternative Nectarines, apricots and plums can be used here in place of the peaches.
Do ensure that the fruits are ripe but not bruised.

Almond, Plum and Strawberry Smoothie

Plums offer a good source of fibre. Red plums also contain beta carotene – the pigment found in foods such as carrots, oranges and dark green vegetables – and an important antioxidant nutrient.

Ingredients

225 g/8 oz ripe plums

300 ml/½ pint bio strawberry yogurt

few drops almond essence

2–3 tsp clear honey, or to taste

2 scoops strawberry ice cream, to serve

1 tbsp toasted flaked almonds, to decorate

Method

Rinse the plums, cut in half, discard the stones and place in a smoothie machine or blender. Spoon the yogurt into the machine and add the almond essence and honey to taste. If using a smoothie machine, blend on mix for 15 seconds and then on smooth for 45 seconds. In a blender, blend for 1–2 minutes or until smooth. Pour into glasses, add a scoop of ice cream to each, sprinkle with the toasted flaked almonds and serve.

Alternative If fresh plums are not available, use a 400 g can of preserved plums.
Drain well and then proceed as above.

Banana Sundae Smoothie

When using bananas in smoothies, do ensure that they are ripe. Under-ripe fruits will not blend well with the other ingredients, and the flavour will be impaired.

Ingredients

2 ripe bananas

150 ml/¹/₄ pint freshly squeezed orange juice

300 ml/¹/₂ pint coconut milk

4 fresh or dried dates, stoned and chopped

2 scoops chocolate ice cream, to serve

2–4 ripe or maraschino cherries, to serve

1 tsp grated chocolate, to decorate

Method

Cut the bananas into chunks and place all the ingredients except the ice cream, the cherries and chocolate in a smoothie machine or blender. If using a smoothie machine, blend on mix for 15 seconds and then on smooth for 45 seconds. In a blender, blend for 1–2 minutes or until smooth. Pour into glasses and add a scoop of ice cream to each. Decorate with the cherries and a sprinkle of chocolate and serve.

Alternative Replace the coconut milk with strawberry flavoured yogurt and use toffee pecan ice cream.

Passionate Peach Melba Smoothie

Like the dessert of the same name, this smoothie is quick and easy to make and tastes even better than it looks. As with all smoothies, it is important to ensure that the fruit you use is in peak condition.

Ingredients

1 ripe passion fruit

3 tbsp mango or orange juice

3–4 ripe peaches, stoned

175 g/6 oz fresh or thawed frozen raspberries

4 scoops vanilla ice cream

wafer biscuits, to serve

Method

Cut the passion fruit in half and scoop out the flesh and seeds. Sieve the flesh if a smoother texture is preferred. Place in a smoothie machine or blender and add the mango or orange juice, peaches, raspberries and two scoops of ice cream. If using a smoothie machine, blend on mix for 15 seconds and then on smooth for 45 seconds. In a blender, blend for 1–2 minutes or until smooth. Pour into glasses and add a scoop of ice cream to each. Top with a wafer and serve.

Alternative Make the smoothie as above, omitting the raspberries but adding more peaches and a little more ice cream. Top with the ice cream, drizzle with raspberry coulis and serve immediately.

Four Fruit Smoothie

Choose your favourite fruits for this smoothie – try and use those that are high in energy giving carbohydrates, such as blackberries, cooking apples, mangos, papayas, pears and raspberries.

Ingredients

100 g/4 oz fresh blackberries

1 ripe mango

1 cooking apple

1 ripe pear, peeled

150 ml/¼ pint coconut milk

4 ice cubes

Method

Hull the blackberries if necessary. Peel and stone the mango, cutting the flesh into chunks, then core the apple and pear and cut into chunks. Place all the fruit in a smoothie machine or blender. Add the coconut milk and ice cubes. If using a smoothie machine, blend on mix for 15 seconds and then on smooth for 45 seconds. In a blender, blend for 1–2 minutes or until smooth. Pour into glasses and serve immediately.

Alternative Replace the coconut milk with live yogurt and stir in two tablespoons of rolled oats.

Real Strawberry Milkshake

Whether or not this transports you back to childhood, once tasted this fabulous shake will have you hooked.

Ingredients

225 g/8 oz ripe strawberries

300 ml/¹/₂ pint chilled semi–skimmed milk

4 ice cubes

2 scoops strawberry flavoured ice cream, to serve

1 tbsp lightly whipped whipping or double cream, to serve

2 extra ripe strawberries, to decorate

Method

Hull the strawberries and rinse lightly. Place in a smoothie machine or blender and add the milk and ice cubes. If using a smoothie machine, blend on mix for 15 seconds and then on smooth for 45 seconds. In a blender, blend for 1–2 minutes or until smooth. Pour into tall glasses and add a scoop of ice cream to each, top with a little whipped cream and decorate with the extra strawberry.

Alternative Other fruits can be used in the same way. Try bananas, raspberries, apricots or pineapple, varying the flavour of ice cream accordingly. Or make a chocolate milkshake by omitting all the fruits and using 2–3 tbsp of melted chocolate.

Mango and Lychee Smoothie

Mango has excellent nutritional properties, being high in fibre and antioxidants and one of the few fruits that contain significant amounts of vitamin E.

Ingredients

2 ripe mangos
300 ml/^{1}/$_2$ pint coconut milk
225 g/8 oz fresh lychees, or 400 g can lychees, drained
2 cardamom pods
4 ice cubes

Method

Peel the mangos and cut the flesh away from the stones. Cut the flesh into slices and place in a smoothie machine or blender together with the coconut milk. Peel and stone the lychees if using fresh, adding to the mango. Crush the cardamom pods and add the seeds to the machine with the ice cubes. If using a smoothie machine, blend on mix for 15 seconds and then on smooth for 45 seconds. In a blender, blend for 1–2 minutes or until smooth. Pour into glasses and serve immediately.

Alternative Peel the lychees over a bowl to catch any juice and add the juice to the machine before blending.

Kiwi with Cucumber with Orange

It really does not matter whether you use green or gold kiwi fruits in this recipe – both will work very well. If you can find blood oranges use these, as they will give a distinctive flavour to this smoothie.

Ingredients

2 ripe kiwi fruits
4 tbsp apple juice
1 hothouse cucumber
2 blood oranges
4 ice cubes
6 tbsp crème fraîche
2 orange twists, to decorate

Method

Peel the kiwi fruits and cut into chunks, then place in a smoothie machine or blender, together with the apple juice. Peel the cucumber, discarding the seeds, chop and add to the machine. Peel the oranges, discarding the bitter white pith and any pips. Add to the machine together with the ice cubes. If using a smoothie machine, blend on mix for 15 seconds and then on smooth for 45 seconds. In a blender, blend for 1–2 minutes or until smooth. Add the crème fraîche and whizz for a further 20 seconds. Pour into glasses and serve decorated with a twist of orange.

Alternative If blood oranges are unavailable, look for a fruit juice made from blood oranges or use traditional-style oranges.

Pear and Date Whizz

Enjoy a refreshing drink that is guaranteed to keep you cool even when the temperature's rising.

Ingredients

3 ripe pears, such as Conference or Williams

6 fresh or dried dates, stoned and chopped

300 ml/^{1}/$_2$ pint bio natural yogurt

2–3 tsp clear honey, or to taste

4–6 ice cubes

Method

Peel the pears, core and chop and place in a smoothie machine or blender. Add the rest of the ingredients, including the ice cubes. If using a smoothie machine, blend on mix for 15 seconds and then on smooth for 45 seconds. In a blender, blend for 1–2 minutes or until smooth. Pour into glasses and serve immediately.

Alternative Replace the natural yogurt and ice cubes with four scoops of vanilla ice cream.

Watermelon Semi-Freddo

This extremely simple and easy to make drink is perfect for any age and superb for long, hot summer days or evenings. If preferred, you can make ahead, freeze, then allow to semi-thaw and use.

Ingredients

¹/₂ watermelon

3 tbsp mango or tropical fruit juice

1 tbsp clear honey, or to taste

100 g/4 oz ripe
    strawberries

4 ice cubes

Method

Discard the skin and seeds from the watermelon and cut the flesh into chunks. Place in a smoothie machine or blender with the mango juice and add honey to taste. Hull the strawberries, rinse lightly and add to the machine with the ice cubes. If using a smoothie machine, blend on mix for 15 seconds and then on smooth for 45 seconds until a 'slush' is formed. In a blender, blend for 1–2 minutes or until the 'slush' is formed. Pour into tall glasses and serve.

Alternative Use other melons according to availability and personal preference, adding 2–3 extra ice cubes to get the 'slushy' texture.

Blackcurrant Granita

When making this granita, turn the freezer setting to rapid freeze in order to speed up the freezing process and obtain the required texture. Don't forget to turn the setting back to normal when finished.

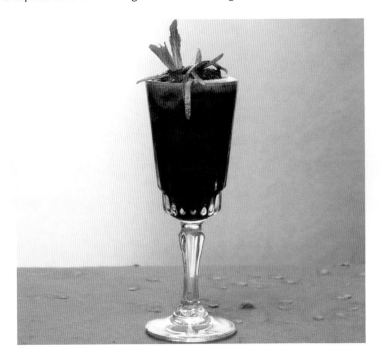

Ingredients

225 g/8 oz fresh blackcurrants

75 g/3 oz fresh redcurrants

4 tbsp blackcurrant cordial

2–3 tsp clear honey, or to taste

1 large or 2 medium juicy eating apples, such as Granny Smith

6 ice cubes

Method

Remove the blackcurrants from their stalks and rinse. Remove redcurrants from the stalks and rinse. Place both currants with the cordial and honey to taste in a smoothie machine or blender. Core the apples and cut into wedges. Add to the machine with the ice cubes. If using a smoothie machine, blend on mix for 15 seconds and then on smooth for 45 seconds. In a blender, blend for 1–2 minutes or until smooth. Pour into a freezeable container and freeze for 1 hour or until slushy. Spoon into glasses and serve immediately.

Alternative Look for all three currants, black, red and white and use an equal amount of each. Add honey to taste.

Greek Delight

Enjoy a taste of the Mediterranean sun with Greek yogurt and plump, lush purple or green figs. There is no need to skin these, but do use ripe fruits and if necessary allow to ripen for a couple of days in a warm room.

Ingredients

4 ripe figs

2–3 tsp clear honey, or to taste

2 large oranges

150 ml/¹/₄ pint Greek yogurt

150 ml/¹/₄ pint semi–skimmed milk

2 scoops vanilla ice cream, to serve

2 mint sprigs, to decorate

Method

Lightly rinse the figs and cut in half, then place in a smoothie machine or blender with honey to taste. Peel the oranges, discarding the bitter white pith, and divide into segments. Add the yogurt and milk. If using a smoothie machine, blend on mix for 15 seconds and then on smooth for 45 seconds. In a blender, blend for 1–2 minutes or until smooth. Pour into glasses, add a scoop of ice cream to each and decorate with a sprig of mint. Serve immediately.

Alternative Use 150 ml/¹/₄ pint freshly squeezed orange juice in place of the whole oranges.

Blueberry Cooler

Blueberries are grown on small, low lying bushes in hot climates such as Umbria and parts of the United States. Recent research has shown that they have strong antioxidant properties, even more so with dried blueberries.

Ingredients

150 g/5 oz fresh blueberries

1–2 tsp caster sugar

150 ml/¹/₄ pint clear apple juice

300 ml/¹/₂ pint live natural yogurt

4 ice cubes

2 scoops raspberry ripple ice cream, to serve

1–2 tbsp dried blueberries, to decorate

2 mint sprigs, to decorate

Method

Rinse the blueberries and place in a smoothie machine or blender with the sugar, apple juice, yogurt and ice cubes. If using a smoothie machine, blend on mix for 15 seconds and then on smooth for 45 seconds. In a blender, blend for 1–2 minutes or until a 'slush' is formed. Pour into glasses, add the ice cream and sprinkle the tops with the dried blueberries. Decorate with the mint sprigs and serve.

Alternative Pour the prepared Blueberry Cooler into a freezeable container and freeze on rapid freeze for 30 minutes or until semi-frozen. Spoon into tall glasses and serve with a long spoon.

Summer Sizzler

When using yogurt in a smoothie take care not to over–blend, as the yogurt can lose its consistency and become quite thin. Therefore when using yogurt with fruits that take a little more effort to blend, add the yogurt towards the end.

Ingredients

1 medium, ripe pineapple

3 tbsp pineapple juice

1 ripe passion fruit

100 g/4 oz fresh strawberries

2–3 tsp clear honey

150 ml/¹/₄ pint bio strawberry yogurt

4 ice cubes

Method

Discard the plume, skin and central core from the pineapple and cut into chunks. Place in a smoothie machine or blender with the pineapple juice. Scoop the flesh and seeds from the passion fruit. Lightly rinse the strawberries and cut any large strawberries in half. Add to the machine with the honey, yogurt and ice cubes. If using a smoothie machine, blend on mix for 15 seconds and then on smooth for 45 seconds. In a blender, blend for 1–2 minutes or until smooth. Pour into glasses and serve immediately.

Alternative Other fruits and flavoured yogurts can be used in place of the strawberries. Try raspberries, blackberries, mango, guava or blueberries.

Caribbean Slush

Enjoy this cooling drink when the heat is up and you are relaxing round a pool, in the garden or just need a cool down.

Ingredients

2 ripe papayas
1 ripe mango
300 ml/¹/₂ pint chilled pineapple juice
small piece root ginger
4 ice cubes

Method

Peel the papaya, discard the seeds and cut the flesh into chunks. Peel the mango and cut the flesh away from the stone, chop the flesh and place in a smoothie machine or blender with the papaya flesh and pineapple juice. Peel the ginger, grate and add to the machine with the ice cubes. If using a smoothie machine, blend on mix for 15 seconds and then on smooth for 45 seconds. In a blender, blend for 1–2 minutes or until a 'slush' is formed. Pour into chilled glasses and serve immediately.

Alternative Replace the root ginger with a little finely grated lime rind and two tablespoons of lime juice.

Orange and Chocolate Smoothie

If, like me, you are a real chocoholic, you will love this smoothie. Do use the best chocolate and ice cream that you can find and don't worry about the calories – you need a treat every now and again.

Ingredients

1 large orange
300 ml/¹/₂ pint chilled semi–skimmed milk
50 g/2 oz good quality plain or milk chocolate, grated
4 scoops chocolate ice cream
1 tbsp chopped mixed nuts, to decorate

Method

Grate 1–2 teaspoons of orange rind from the orange and reserve. Peel the orange, discarding the bitter white pith, and divide into segments. Place the orange rind and segments in a smoothie machine or blender with the milk and grated chocolate and two scoops of ice cream. If using a smoothie machine, blend on mix for 15 seconds and then on smooth for 45 seconds. In a blender, blend for 1–2 minutes or until smooth. Pour into glasses and add a scoop of ice cream to each, sprinkle with the nuts and serve.

Alternative Use vanilla ice cream in place of the chocolate ice cream and sprinkle with a little grated chocolate before serving.

Apricots with Peaches and Almonds

This has faint overtones of marzipan, thanks to the addition of a little almond essence. If preferred, omit this and use vanilla extract or 1 teaspoon of finely grated orange or lemon rind.

Ingredients

225 g/8 oz ripe apricots
2 ripe peaches
4 tbsp mango juice
$^1/_2$ tsp almond essence
4 ice cubes
2 scoops vanilla ice cream, to serve
1 tbsp toasted flaked almonds, to decorate

Method

Lightly rinse the apricots and peaches, cut in half and discard the stones. Place in a smoothie machine or blender with the mango juice, almond essence and ice cubes. If using a smoothie machine, blend on mix for 15 seconds and then on smooth for 45 seconds. In a blender, blend for 1–2 minutes or until smooth. Pour into glasses. Top each with a scoop of ice cream, sprinkle with the toasted flaked almonds and serve.

Alternative   Nectarines can be used in place of the peaches. If they are not available, use ripe mangos, papayas or even well-drained, canned peaches, canned in fruit juice rather than syrup.

Toffee and Chocolate Smoothie

This is definitely an indulgent smoothie – so have it in the summer when you can go for a walk to work off the excess calories.

Ingredients

300 ml/½ pint toffee flavoured yogurt
150 ml/¼ pint chilled semi-skimmed milk
4 scoops vanilla ice cream
2 rolled wafer biscuits, to serve
1 tsp crumbled chocolate flake, to decorate

Method

Place the yogurt, milk and two scoops of the ice cream in a smoothie machine or blender. If using a smoothie machine, blend on mix for 15 seconds and then on smooth for 45 seconds. In a blender, blend for 1–2 minutes or until smooth. Pour into chilled glasses and add the remaining scoop of ice cream to each along with a wafer biscuit. Sprinkle with the chocolate flake and serve.

Alternative Use a different flavoured yogurt in place of the toffee: try raspberry, cherry or peach and passion fruit.

Cocktails and Punches

At the end of a busy day we all need to unwind, and what better way than with a long and relaxing drink, perhaps sitting outside in the cool of the evening in summer. Or in the winter, enjoy a warming glass of punch full of the aroma of fragrant spices. Sometimes a creamy, smooth cocktail hits the spot, or perhaps try a spicy cocktail to wake up the taste buds. Alternatively, simply enjoy a delicious non-alcoholic drink to relax the mind and body after a stressful day's work.

When entertaining it is customary to offer a drink before eating. This can simply be a glass of wine or fruit juice, but as a change why not surprise your family and friends and offer something different. During the winter serve a glass of fragrant, warming Cherry and Madeira Punch. Or in the summer wow your guests with Tropical Bubbles. Whatever your choice, there are plenty of ideas here, guaranteed to please the senses and delight the taste buds. The cocktails and tall drinks in this section serve two, the punches six to eight – so get shaking!

Iced Pimms

Pimms conjures up the thought of long, hot summer days or evenings, friends coming round and relaxing on a terrace, watching the kids play or simply just sitting.

Ingredients

small piece cucumber
$1/_2$ small orange, preferably organic
$1/_2$ lemon, preferably organic
$1/_2$ small eating apple
6 strawberries
few raspberries or seedless grapes
few mint sprigs
300 ml/$1/_2$ pint Pimms
900 ml/1 $1/_2$ pints lemonade
6–10 ice cubes

Method

Rinse the cucumber and chop into small pieces. Rinse the orange and lemon and cut into small wedges. Rinse the apple, core and chop. Rinse the strawberries and slice. Rinse the raspberries or grapes. Place all the fruits in a tall jug, then pour in the Pimms and stir. Add the lemonade, then the ice cubes, allow to stand for 5 minutes then stir and pour into glasses and serve, spooning a little fruit into each glass.

Alternative For an extra kick, add 75–150 ml/3–5 fl oz gin to the jug after adding the Pimms.

Mint Julep

Julep is derived from the Turkish word julab meaning 'rose water', and was a sugar syrup used as a means of taking medicines. By the 1800s, juleps were popular in America where they developed into the drink that is still made today. Americans usually add bourbon to their juleps, but this is a non–alcoholic version.

Ingredients
50 g/2 oz granulated sugar
8 tbsp water
crushed ice
4–6 mint sprigs
100 ml/4 fl oz elderflower cordial
mint sprigs, to decorate

Method
Place the sugar in a heavy based saucepan and add the water. Place over a gentle heat and heat gently, stirring until the sugar has dissolved. Bring to the boil and boil for 3 minutes or until a light syrup has formed. Remove and allow to cool. Crush the mint sprigs. Add sufficient crushed ice to half-fill two tall glasses and pour in the sugar syrup and elderflower cordial. Add the crushed mint, stir well and serve immediately decorated with a mint sprig and a stirrer.

Alternative   Make an alcoholic julep by substituting the elderflower cordial with bourbon or whisky.

Mandarin Highball

Highballs became popular in the United States, especially New York, at the end of the nineteenth century. It is a long drink speedily prepared by simply pouring the ingredients over crushed ice into tall glasses.

Ingredients

crushed ice

120 ml/4 fl oz Mandarin Napoleon

50 ml/2 fl oz mandarin juice

dash Angostura Bitters

200 ml/7 fl oz bitter lemon

Method

Half–fill a tall glass with crushed ice, then pour over the Mandarin Napoleon, the mandarin juice and a dash of Angostura Bitters. Stir, then pour in the bitter lemon and serve with a stirrer.

Alternative For a less alcoholic version, replace the Mandarin Napoleon with orange juice and add 2–3 extra dashes of Angostura Bitters.

Pineapple Velvet

When choosing glasses for cocktails, there are many different varieties. Traditional cocktail glasses contain 150 ml/5 fl oz and are normally triangle in shape. Of course if it is a Champagne cocktail being served, as here, then a Champagne flute is the perfect glass.

Ingredients

120 ml/4 fl oz lager, chilled
50 ml/2 fl oz pineapple juice, chilled
120 ml/4 fl oz Champagne, chilled
small wedges of pineapple, to decorate

Method

Pour the lager into a glass, add the pineapple juice and stir. Top up with the Champagne, decorate with a wedge of pineapple and serve.

Alternative Use ginger beer in place of the lager and sparkling wine in place of the Champagne.
Stir and serve with a small wedge of pineapple.

Tropical Bubbles

This delicious drink is crammed full of ripe, plump Caribbean fruits. For maximum flavour, chill the fruits for a short while before using.

Ingredients

1 large, ripe mango
1 large, ripe papaya
2 ripe guavas
150 ml/$^1/_4$ pint pineapple juice
$^1/_2$ bottle chilled Champagne or sparkling wine

Method

Peel the mango, papaya and guavas and discard the stone and seeds. Cut into chunks. Place in a blender and add the pineapple juice. Whizz for 1–2 minutes or until smooth, then pour into chilled tall glasses and top up with Champagne. Serve with a stirrer.

Alternative For a non-alcoholic verion, omit the Champagne and use sparkling spring water or lemonade.

Rum and Guava Fizz

When serving cocktails, a nice touch is to frost the glasses. It is really quite simple. Place some caster sugar in a saucer about 5 mm/¹/₄ inch thick. Rub around the rim of the glass with either water, orange or lemon juice and dip immediately into the sugar. Leave for a few minutes to set before adding the drink.

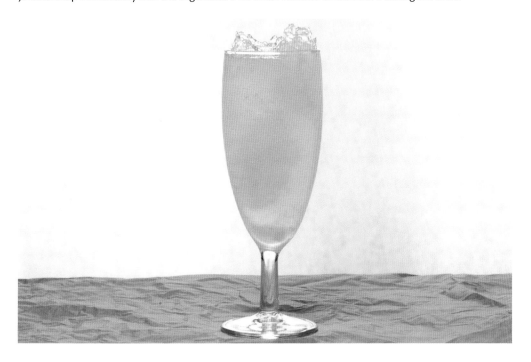

Ingredients

3 ripe guavas

150 ml/¹/₄ pint rum, preferably white rum

50 ml/2 fl oz pineapple juice

crushed ice

¹/₂ bottle sparkling white wine

Method

Peel the guavas and discard the seeds. Pass through a juicer into a jug, then stir in the rum and pineapple juice. Place some crushed ice into tall glasses, pour over the guava mixture, top up with the sparkling wine and serve.

Alternative Replace the sparkling wine with sparkling apple juice, lemonade or mineral water and use a few dashes of Angostura Bitters in place of the rum.

Bloody Mary with a Twist

This must be the most well-known of all cocktails, but this one has a twist. You will need to plan ahead in order to be able to make this, but it is well worth the extra effort.

Ingredients

2–3 medium chillies, such as serrano or jalapeño
1 bottle vodka
225 g/8 oz ripe tomatoes
few dashes Tabasco sauce
crushed ice
twist of lemon and 2 celery sticks, to serve

Method

Make a slit down the length of each chilli and discard the seeds. Place in the bottle of vodka, screw down and leave overnight or longer if time permits. Pass the tomatoes through a juicer into a jug and add Tabasco sauce to taste. Place some crushed ice into two glasses and pour over 25– 50ml/1–2 fl oz of the chilli-flavoured vodka. Top up with the tomato juice and add a twist of lemon. Place the celery stick in the glasses to use as a stirrer. Please note that the longer the chillies are left in the vodka, the stronger the flavour and heat will be.

Alternative Make a Virgin Mary by omitting the vodka. Flavour the fresh tomato juice with chilli by adding $^1/_2$ deseeded chilli when juicing the tomatoes. Add a few dashes of Worcestershire sauce in place of the Tabasco sauce.

Campari Delight

Cocktails are generally served before a meal, and it is quite normal to serve nibbles to help to alleviate the effects of the alcohol prior to eating. Crisps and salsa would go well with this recipe.

Ingredients

1 large, ripe mango
150 ml/^{1}/$_4$ pint freshly squeezed orange juice
120 ml/4 fl oz Campari
150ml/^{1}/$_4$ pint mango juice
crushed ice
orange twists, to decorate
2 long cinnamon sticks for stirring

Method

Peel the mango and cut the flesh away from the stone. Pass through a juicer into a jug. Mix the mango and orange juice together and stir in the Campari. Place some crushed ice in glasses then pour over the prepared cocktail. Fix an orange twist on the side of each glass, add a cinnamon stick to use as a stirrer and serve immediately.

Alternative For a non-alcoholic version, increase the mango and orange juice each to 200 ml/7 fl oz and omit the Campari. Add 2–3 tbsp of lime juice and a few dashes of Tabasco sauce.

Spiced Fruit Punch

This deliciously different drink is perfect either for a warm summer's evening or a cold winter's night.

Ingredients

300 ml/¹/₂ pt orange and mango juice

thinly pared rind of 2 lemons

50 ml/2 fl oz lemon juice

3 whole cloves

1 large cinnamon stick, bruised

¹/₂ tsp ground allspice

600 ml/1 pt chilled ginger ale

1 small ripe mango, peeled, stoned and finely chopped

crushed ice

Method

Place the fruit juices in a large jug and stir in the spices. Allow to stand in the refrigerator for at least 2 hours, stirring occasionally. When ready to serve, stir in the ginger ale and chopped mango and serve over crushed ice.

Alternative If liked, the punch can be served warm. Heat the fruit juices with the spices over a very gentle heat. When almost at boiling point, remove from the heat and carefully pour into a punch bowl. Gradually pour in the ginger ale and serve in heatproof glasses with cinnamon sticks to stir.

Apple Soda Cup

For many of these drinks and particularly during the summer months, you will need a regular supply of crushed ice. To make, simply whizz some ice cubes in a blender. To save damaging your machine, break up the larger pieces of ice slightly before crushing. Once made, use immediately or as soon as possible as it will quickly melt.

Ingredients

2 ripe eating apples, such as Granny Smith

2–3 star anise, lightly bashed

1 cinnamon stick, bruised

1 lemon, preferably organic

4 tbsp granulated sugar

1.2 litres/2 pints clear apple juice

600 ml/1 pint soda water, to serve

Method

Peel, core and slice the apples and place in a bowl with the star anise and cinnamon stick. Pare a thin strip from the lemon and squeeze out the juice. Add to the apples and stir. Sprinkle over the sugar. Heat 300 ml/$^1/_2$ pint of the apple juice to just below boiling then pour over the apples and leave to cool. Once cool, pour the remaining apple juice over the mixture. Half-fill tall glasses with the drink, add a couple of apple slices and top up with the soda water. Serve.

Alternative For an alcoholic version replace the apple juice with dry cider or a mixture of both. Or if liked, add 150 ml/1/4 pint Calvados brandy before heating.

Summer Sparkle

Whether you use a Champagne or sparkling wine, this 'fizz' will definitely put a sparkle in your eyes and a spring in your step.

Ingredients

4 ripe strawberries

4 tsp grenadine

2–3 tbsp brandy

1 bottle Champagne or sparkling wine, chilled

ice cubes, optional

Method

Lightly rinse the strawberries and hull if preferred. Place a strawberry into four tall Champagne flutes. Add a teaspoon of grenadine to each with brandy to taste and stir. Top up with the Champagne or sparkling wine and serve, with ice cubes if preferred.

Alternative Replace the Champagne or sparkling wine with half elderflower and apple juice and half sparkling mineral water. Or if preferred, use pink Champagne and omit the grenadine.

Honeysuckle Cup

To host a drinks party it is not necessary to have an abundance of equipment: the most important items are, of course, the glasses. For garden or patio parties, many people favour plastic glasses, and with children in mind this is an excellent idea. This drink would be perfect for such an occasion.

Ingredients

1 bottle white wine, such as Pinot Grigio, chilled

3–5 tsp clear honey, warmed

2 tbsp Benedictine

150 ml/¼ pint brandy

600 ml/1 pint lemonade

1 ripe peach, sliced

crushed ice

2–4 honeysuckle flowers, to decorate

Method

Pour the wine into a bowl, drizzle in the honey and stir well. Add the Benedictine, brandy and lemonade and stir before adding the peach slices and ice. Check there are no aphids on the flowers and rinse lightly. Float on top of the bowl and serve.

Alternative For a non-alcoholic drink, omit all the alcohol and replace with ginger beer and chilled, freshly brewed green tea.

Pineapple and Ginger Beer Punch

In the late 18th and 19th centuries, punches and cups were served in highly ornate glass bowls, which had matching glasses with handles that hung round the edge of the bowl. Although a nice idea, these days the drink will taste just as good if served in an ordinary glass bowl or glass.

Ingredients

450 ml/³/₄ pint pineapple juice
600 ml/1 pint ginger beer
2–3 tsp clear honey, or to taste
1 small orange, sliced, preferably organic
1 small lime, sliced, preferably organic
3 slices pineapple, fresh or canned, chopped into chunks
few mint sprigs, lightly crushed
crushed ice, to serve
soda water, to serve

Method

Pour the pineapple juice and ginger beer into a large bowl and stir in the honey. Add the sliced fruits. Stir well and add the mint sprigs. Leave for at least 15 minutes for the flavours to develop. Place crushed ice into glasses and half fill with the prepared punch. Top up with the soda water and serve.

Alternative To make this cup alcoholic, add 300 ml/¹/₂ pint dry sherry.

Midsummer Cup

Don't keep this just for midsummer – make it for any occasion throughout the summer months.
Vary the fruits according to personal taste and availability – choose from plums, damsons, greengages,
peaches and white nectarines.

Ingredients

1 bottle dry white wine such as Chardonnay, chilled

1 bottle red wine, such as Beaujolais, chilled

50 ml/2 fl oz Grand Marnier or Cointreau

1–2 tbsp clear honey, or to taste

small wedge melon

small stem grapes

8 strawberries

crushed ice, to serve

600 ml/1 pint soda water, to serve

Method

Pour the wines into a glass bowl, add the Grand Marnier
or Cointreau and honey and stir until the honey has
dissolved. Discard the skin and seeds from the melon and
cut into small chunks. Rinse the grapes and remove their
stalks, then lightly rinse the strawberries and cut in half or
quarters depending on their size. Add to the bowl. To
serve, place some crushed ice into glasses, half fill with
the drink and top up with soda water.

Alternative For a non-alcoholic version, replace the wines with apple juice and ginger ale, and the Grand Marnier
with orange juice and half a teaspoon of finely grated orange rind.

Chocolate Cappuccino Smoothie

This is the perfect end to a delicious meal. If you have an espresso machine with a frother this will speed up the preparation time, but it is not strictly necessary – a balloon whisk will work well.

Ingredients

50 ml/2 fl oz strong black coffee, freshly brewed
2 tsp good quality drinking chocolate
2 tbsp brandy, whisky or rum
1–2 tsp demerara sugar, or to taste
150 ml/¹/₄ pint milk
1 tsp grated chocolate

Method

Pour the hot coffee into a large, wide–necked cup and stir in the drinking chocolate with the brandy, whisky or rum, sugar to taste and your choice of spirit. Heat the milk to just below boiling then either froth or whizz with a balloon whisk until frothy. Pour into the coffee, sprinkle with the grated chocolate and serve.

Alternative To make a non–alcoholic cappuccino, simply omit the alcohol.

Chilled Café Fraîche

Iced coffee makes a refreshing change and is welcome in hot weather at any time of the day or night. The beauty of this recipe is that it is ready in just a few minutes and takes no effort at all.

Ingredients

300 ml/^{1}/$_2$ pint espresso or freshly brewed black
   filter coffee

1–2 tsp demerara sugar, or to taste

150 ml/^{1}/$_4$ pint whole or semi–skimmed milk

4 ice cubes

4 tbsp crème fraîche, to serve

pinch of ground cinnamon or grated chocolate,
   to decorate

cinnamon sticks, to stir

Method

Pour the coffee into a blender and add the sugar. Blend until the sugar has dissolved – about 15 seconds. Add the milk and ice cubes and blend for a further 25 seconds or until frothy. Pour into large–necked cups, top with crème fraîche and sprinkle the top with a little ground cinnamon or grated chocolate. Add a cinnamon stick to use as a stirrer.

Alternative   For a kick, add 2 tbsp brandy, whisky or Cointreau when blending.

Summer Berry Cooler

Use plump, ripe fruits that are undamaged for this recipe. If liked, clean and prepare the fruits ahead of time, keep in a box in the refrigerator and then quickly whizz whenever required.

Ingredients

450 ml/³/₄ pint cranberry and raspberry juice

150 ml/¹/₄ pint elderflower cordial

225 g/8 oz mixed berries, such as strawberries, loganberries and raspberries, hulled and rinsed

3–4 crushed mint sprigs

2–3 tsp clear honey, or to taste

crushed ice, to serve

Method

Pour the cranberry and raspberry juice and elderflower cordial into a bowl and add all the cleaned fruits. Add the crushed mint sprigs and honey, stir and leave to stand for 30 minutes to allow the flavours to develop. Place crushed ice in tall glasses then pour over the drink. Serve immediately.

Alternative Add 85 ml/3 fl oz cherry brandy or peach schnapps to the fruit juice and, if liked, replace the berries with sliced fresh peaches, nectarines and fresh cherries.

Passion Fruit and Vodka Smoothie

Vodka does not have much, if any, flavour and takes on the flavours that it is blended with. Here the vodka has been teamed with passion fruit and orange to create a refreshing smoothie with a bit of a kick.

Ingredients

2 ripe passion fruits

1 large orange

1–2 tsp clear honey, or to taste

150 ml/¹/₄ pint coconut milk

150 ml/¹/₄ pint natural live yogurt

120 ml/4 fl oz vodka

6 ice cubes

Method

Cut the passion fruits in half and scoop out the flesh and seeds. Sieve the fruit if a smoother texture is preferred and reserve the juice. Peel the orange, discarding the bitter white pith, and divide into segments. Place all the ingredients including the ice cubes into a smoothie machine or blender. If using a smoothie machine, blend on mix for 10 seconds and then on smooth for 30 seconds. If using a blender, whizz for 1–2 minutes or until smooth. Pour into glasses and serve.

Alternative For a non-alcoholic smoothie, replace the vodka with ginger ale or ginger beer and stir in after blending the other ingredients.

Purple Cream Cocktail

If you have trouble finding coconut milk, make your own from coconut cream. Break off about 1 tablespoon of the coconut cream and grate. Add an equal amount (or slightly less) of caster sugar, then pour on sufficient hot water to dissolve the sugar and coconut, forming milk. Use it all as it will not keep.

Ingredients

150 ml/¼ pint coconut milk
50 ml/2 fl oz blackcurrant cordial
120 ml/4 fl oz ginger ale
1–2 tsp clear honey
150 ml/¼ pint pineapple juice
crushed ice
fresh blackcurrants, to decorate

Method

Place all the ingredient except the fresh blackcurrants in a smoothie machine or cocktail shaker. If using a smoothie machine, blend on mix for 15 seconds, or shake in a cocktail shaker for 45 seconds or until smooth. Pour into glasses and serve decorated with fresh blackcurrants.

Alternative For an alcoholic cocktail replace the ginger ale with white rum and use assis in place of the blackcurrant cordial.

Fruity Wake-Up

Many drink recipes refer to measures and not to an actual amount. This can be confusing, especially if you do not possess a cocktail shaker, where the lid has the measures engraved on it. For future reference, a measure is 25 ml/1 fl oz and is easy to measure with the aid of a measuring jug or even a measuring spoon.

Ingredients

1 large, ripe pear
6 ready-to-eat dried prunes
1 large orange
150 ml/¼ pint apple juice
150 ml/¼ pint orange juice
crushed ice, to serve
soda water, to serve

Method

Peel and core the pear, cut into chunks and reserve. Cut the prunes into small pieces. Peel the orange, discarding the bitter white pith, and divide into segments. Put all the ingredients except the crushed ice and soda water in a smoothie machine or blender. If using a smoothie machine, blend on mix for 15 seconds and then on smooth for 45 seconds. If using a blender, whizz for 1–2 minutes or until smooth. Place some crushed ice into tall glasses, pour over the blended fruits and top up with soda water.

Alternative Make this a wake-up for any time of day or night by adding 85 ml/3 fl oz Grand Marnier and 1 tsp of finely grated orange rind before blending.

Spicy Mary

If liked, you could decorate the rim of the glasses for this recipe. Place some salt in a saucer to a depth of 5 mm/¼ inch. Rub the rim of the glass with a little lemon or lime juice then dip in the salt, allowing to set before using.

Ingredients

225 g/8 oz ripe tomatoes, chopped
2 tsp freshly snipped chives
2 tsp freshly chopped coriander
1 tsp finely grated lemon rind
¹/₂ small jalapeno chilli, deseeded
few shakes Worcestershire sauce
ice cubes
150 ml/¹/₄ pint ginger beer
celery sticks, for stirring

Method

Place all the ingredients except the ice cubes, ginger beer and celery sticks into a smoothie machine or a blender. If using a smoothie machine, blend on mix for 15 seconds and then on smooth for 45 seconds. If using a blender, whizz for 1–2 minutes or until smooth. Place the ice cubes in tall glasses, half-fill with the Spicy Mary and top up with ginger beer. Serve with a celery stick to use as a stirrer.

Alternative Replace the ginger beer with vodka and wait for the buzz!

Whisky with a Twist

When using whisky in a cocktail, use the blended varieties as they offer excellent value for money. Save the malt whiskies to drink by themselves.

Ingredients

1 small wedge of melon, such as ogen or cantaloupe
1 small orange
120 ml/4 fl oz whisky
4 tbsp ginger wine
2 tbsp crushed ice, to serve
2 orange twists, to decorate

Method

Discard the skin and seeds from the melon and cut into chunks. Peel the orange, discarding the bitter white pith, and divide into segments. Place the fruits with the whisky and ginger wine in a smoothie machine or blender. If using a smoothie machine, blend on mix for 15 seconds and then on smooth for 45 seconds. If using a blender, whizz for 1–2 minutes or until smooth. Place the crushed ice in glasses. Pour over the whisky mixture, decorate the glasses with a twist of orange and serve.

Alternative Replace the whisky with more ginger wine.

Pink Gin Granita

The pink in a 'Pink Gin' comes from Angostura Bitters, which were originally derived from plant extracts as a remedy for digestive and stomach problems. The British Navy added it to their medicine chest but quickly discovered an alternative use for it!

Ingredients

150 ml/¹/₄ pint gin

¹/₂–1 tsp Angostura Bitters

200 ml/7 fl oz smooth orange juice

2 tsp clear honey

twists of orange and redcurrant sprigs if available, to decorate

spoons, to serve

Method

Set the freezer to rapid freeze at least 1 hour before the granita is required. Pour the gin, Angostura Bitters, orange juice and honey in a blender or cocktail shaker and blend or shake until mixed. Pour into a shallow, freezeable container and freeze for about 1 hour or until semi-frozen. Break up into small ice crystals and spoon into glasses. Place a spoon in each, decorate with a twist of orange and redcurrant sprigs if using, and serve immediately.

Alternative Replace the gin with red grapefruit juice for a non-alcoholic version. Do remember to return the freezer to its correct setting after finishing freezing.

Celery and Cucumber Martini

Whether you shake or stir this martini, once you have offered one to your friends, be prepared to make plenty more.

Ingredients

2 young celery sticks

$^1/_2$ hothouse cucumber

few sprigs mint

150 ml/$^1/_4$ pint white Bacardi

50 ml/2 fl oz white Vermouth

crushed ice, to serve

2–4 green olives, to decorate

Method

Trim the celery of all the leaves. Cut into small chunks. Peel the cucumber, cut in half and discard the seeds. Chop. Place all the ingredients except the crushed ice and olives in a smoothie machine or blender. If using a smoothie machine, blend on mix for 15 seconds and then on smooth for 45 seconds. If using a blender, whizz for 1–2 minutes or until smooth. Place crushed ice in glasses, pour over the cocktail and serve immediately with the olives on cocktail sticks.

Alternative Replace the white Bacardi and white Vermouth with ginger beer for a non-alcoholic version.

Hot Spicy Cider

Grenadine is a cordial with very little or no alcohol content, depending on what brand you buy, and is made from the sweetened juice of pomegranates. It is used mainly for sweetening and colouring, as it has a glorious red colour.

Ingredients

600 ml/1 pint cider

25 ml/1 fl oz grenadine

15 g/1 oz light muscovado sugar

4 whole cloves

2 star anise

small cinnamon stick

few whole allspice, or 1 tsp ground allspice

Method

Pour the cider and grenadine into a heatproof bowl and add the sugar and all the spices. Place over a pan of gently simmering water and heat, stirring occasionally for about 12–15 minutes or until the sugar has dissolved. Strain into heatproof glasses and serve.

Alternative Replace the cider with clear apple juice. If liked the ingredients can be heated in a heavy based saucepan, but take care not to allow the drink to boil.

Cherry and Madeira Punch

If you often serve hot drinks it would be worth investing in some heat resistant glasses with handles, making it far easier to pick up the hot drink.

Ingredients

1 bottle Madeira or port

2 tbsp cherry brandy

150 ml/¹/₄ pint Kirsch

600 ml/1 pint red grapefruit juice

2 tbsp clear honey

2 cinnamon sticks, bruised

soda water, optional

maraschino cherries, optional

Method

Pour the Madeira or port with the cherry brandy and Kirsch into a heatproof bowl and heat for 12–15 minutes or until hot. Stir in the grapefruit juice and add the honey and cinnamon sticks. Heat for a further 8–10 minutes then ladle into heatproof glasses and dilute with soda water if liked. Hang a couple of cherries over the rim of the glass if liked and serve.

Alternative For a non-alcoholic version, replace the maraschino cherries with fresh cherries, use red grape juice in place of the Madeira and use apple juice and grenadine in place of the Kirsch and cherry brandy.

Mulled Wine

Mulled wine is a traditional winter drink and is enjoyed by many, especially if living in cold, snowy climates. Heating wine with sugar and spices tends to make it stronger in flavour and increase the impact of the alcohol – so take care!

Ingredients

300 ml/$^1/_2$ pint water

75–100 g/3–4 oz light muscovado sugar

4 whole cloves

2 star anise

4 cardamom pods

2 cinnamon sticks

2 lemon grass stalks

1 bottle red wine, such as a claret or burgundy

150 ml/$^1/_4$ pint rum or brandy

1 small orange, preferably organic

1 small lime, preferably organic

Method

Place the water and sugar in a heavy based saucepan and heat, stirring occasionally until the sugar dissolves. Add the whole cloves and star anise. Lightly bash the cardamom pods and add the seeds to the pan. Lightly bash the cinnamon sticks. Remove the outer leaves from the lemon grass stalks and lightly bash the inner stalk. Add both to the pan together with the red wine and rum or brandy. Slice the orange and lime, add to the bowl then heat for 12–15 minutes or until hot. Strain into a warmed, heatproof bowl and serve immediately.

Alternative Replace the wine with red grape juice and use ginger ale in place of the rum or brandy.

Egg Nog

This is a favourite drink around Christmas and the New Year and was very popular in the 1960s.
Do make sure that the eggs used are very fresh and drink as soon as possible after making.

Ingredients

150 ml/^{1}/$_4$ pint milk

2 medium eggs, separated

50 g/2 oz golden caster sugar

^{1}/$_2$ tsp freshly grated nutmeg

4 tbsp single cream

4–6 tbsp ginger ale

Method

Pour the milk into a non–stick milk pan and bring to just
below boiling point. Meanwhile whisk the egg yolks with
the sugar and freshly grated nutmeg until thick and
creamy, then slowly fold in the single cream before
stirring in the hot milk and ginger ale. Whisk the egg
whites until stiff and soft peaks are formed. Fold the egg
whites into the milk and egg yolk mixture, spoon into
warm glasses and serve with a spoon. If liked grate a little
extra nutmeg over the top.

Alternative For alcoholic Egg Nog add 2–3 tbsp brandy and 2–3 tbsp rum or sherry and proceed as above.

Mulled Ale

Ale was one of the staple drinks for people in the 18th century, including very young children and even babies. Mulled ale was very popular in helping to keep warm. Traditionally, in order to heat the drink, a fire poker was heated until glowing, then placed in the hot ale and left until the sizzling stopped.

Ingredients

$^{1}/_{2}$ lemon, preferably organic

2–3 whole cloves

1 litre/1 $^{3}/_{4}$ pints ale

1 small piece root ginger

freshly grated nutmeg

50–75 g/2–3 oz light muscovado sugar

150 ml/$^{1}/_{4}$ pint brandy

50 ml/2 fl oz rum

Method

Finely grate the rind from the lemon and squeeze out the juice. Place both in a heavy based saucepan and add the remaining ingredients. Heat gently, stirring occasionally until the sugar has dissolved. Heat for 10 minutes or until very hot but not boiling. Strain into a heatproof bowl or glasses and serve.

Alternative For a non-alcoholic version, omit the wine and brandy and replace with ginger beer.

Caribbean Toddy

A 'toddy' is normally associated with Scotch whisky, but in fact as long as the drink has some spirit, a hint of a citrus fruit and sweetness, it is entitled to be called a toddy.

Ingredients

120 ml/4 fl oz white rum
1 tsp demerara sugar
150 ml/$^1/_4$ pint boiling water
6 drops Angostura Bitters
$^1/_2$ tsp finely grated lime rind
2 lime twists, to decorate
freshly grated nutmeg, to decorate

Method

Pour the white rum into a blender or cocktail shaker and add the sugar. Pour over the boiling water and blend or shake until dissolved. Add the Angostura Bitters and shake again until mixed. Pour into heatproof glasses, add a lime twist to each, sprinkle with a little grated nutmeg and serve.

Alternative For a non-alcoholic version, replace the white rum with freshly brewed, hot black tea.

Southern Belle

A swizzle stick would be just the right accompaniment for this stylish drink. Look for sugar swizzle sticks, which are sticks about 10 cm/4 inch in length with crystallized sugar swirled on one end.

Ingredients

85 ml/3 fl oz Southern Comfort
85 ml/3 fl oz peach brandy, or plain brandy
85 ml/3 fl oz double cream
2 dashes Angostura Bitters
few slices of fresh peach
2 swizzle sticks, optional

Method

Place all the ingredients except the fresh peach slices in a blender or cocktail shaker. Blend or shake for 1 minute, then pour into cocktail glasses and decorate with peach slices and swizzle sticks if using. Serve immediately.

Alternative Replace the Southern Comfort with ginger ale and the peach brandy with puréed peach flesh.

Banana Rum Shake

Bananas and coconuts are a common ingredient in Thailand and grow profusely in the hot, humid climate. The addition of the rum adds a kick to the shake, one not to be underestimated.

Ingredients

1 large, ripe banana

150 ml/^{1}/$_4$ pint orange juice

300 ml/^{1}/$_2$ pint coconut milk

1–2 tsp clear honey, or to taste

85 ml/3 fl oz white or dark rum

4 ice cubes

2 scoops vanilla ice cream, to serve

freshly grated nutmeg, to decorate

Method

Peel the banana and cut into chunks. Place in a smoothie machine or blender with the orange juice. Add the coconut milk, honey to taste, the rum and ice cubes. If using a smoothie machine, blend on mix for 15 seconds and then on smooth for 45 seconds. Blend in a blender for 1–2 minutes or until smooth. Pour into glasses and add a scoop of ice cream to each. Sprinkle the tops with a little freshly grated nutmeg and serve immediately.

Alternative For a non-alcoholic version, omit the rum and increase the orange juice by 85 ml/3 fl oz. Use a little grated chocolate in place of the nutmeg.

Index